Kelley Wingate Reading Comprehension and Skills

First Grade

Credits
Content Editor: Jeanette M. Ritch, M.S. Ed.
Copy Editor: Christine Schwab

Visit *carsondellosa.com* for correlations to Common Core, state, national, and Canadian provincial standards.

Carson-Dellosa Publishing, LLC
PO Box 35665
Greensboro, NC 27425 USA
carsondellosa.com

ISBN 978-1-4838-0492-7

02-139141151

Table of Contents

Introduction

Reading proficiency is as much a result of regular practice as anything. This book was developed to help students practice and master the basic skills necessary to become competent readers.

The skills covered within the activity pages of this book are necessary for successful reading comprehension. Many of the activities will build and reinforce vocabulary, the foundation of reading comprehension. These activities lead to practice with more advanced comprehension skills. Then, students begin to answer comprehension questions based on specific reading passages.

The intent of this book is to strengthen students' foundation in reading basics so that they can advance to more challenging reading work.

Common Core State Standards (CCSS) Alignment

This book supports standards-based instruction and is aligned to the CCSS. The standards are listed at the top of each page for easy reference. To help you meet instructional, remediation, and individualization goals, consult the Common Core State Standards alignment chart on page 4.

Leveled Reading Activities

Instructional levels in this book vary. Each area of the book offers multilevel reading activities so that learning can progress naturally. There are three levels, signified by one, two, or three dots at the bottom of the page:

- Level I: These activities will offer the most support.
- Level II: Some supportive measures are built in.
- Level III: Students will understand the concepts and be able to work independently.

All children learn at their own rate. Use your own judgment for introducing concepts to children when developmentally appropriate.

Hands-On Learning

Review is an important part of learning. It helps to ensure that skills are not only covered but internalized. The flash cards at the back of this book will offer endless opportunities for review. Use them for a basic vocabulary drill, or to play bingo or other fun games.

There is also a certificate template at the back of this book for use as students excel at daily assignments or when they finish a unit.

Common Core State Standards Alignment Chart

Common Core State Standards*		Practice Page(s)
Reading Standards for Literature		
Key Ideas and Details	1.RL.1–1.RL.3	5–13, 17–22
Craft and Structure	1.RL.4–1.RL.6	14–16
Integration of Knowledge and Ideas	1.RL.7, 1.RL.9	17–25
Range of Reading and Level of Text Complexity	1.RL.10	5–16, 18–19, 21–25, 59
Reading Standards for Informational Text		
Key Ideas and Details	1.RI.1–1.RI.3	26–34
Craft and Structure	1.RI.5–1.RI.6	35–37
Integration of Knowledge and Ideas	1.RI.7–1.RI.9	38–40
Range of Reading and Level of Text Complexity	1.RI.10	26–34, 39–40, 58, 61
Reading Standards: Foundational Skills		
Print Concepts	1.RF.1	41–46
Phonological Awareness	1.RF.2	47–49
Phonics and Word Recognition	1.RF.3	50–52
Fluency	1.RF.4	53–61
Writing Standards		
Text Types and Purposes	1.W.1–1.W.3	62–70
Production and Distribution of Writing	1.W.5–1.W.6	71–73
Research to Build and Present Knowledge	1.W.7–1.W.8	71–73
Language Standards		
Conventions of Standard English	1.L.1–1.L.2	41–46, 74–91,98–103
Vocabulary Acquisition and Use	1.L.4–1.L.6	80–82, 92–97

Name ______________________________

I.RL.I, I.RL.3, I.RL.I0

Reading Comprehension: Fiction

Read the story. Answer the questions.

Judy's New Doll

Judy has a new doll.

The doll's name is Mika.

Mika and Judy have blue eyes and brown hair.

I. What does Judy have?

____

2. Who is Mika?

____

3. Who has blue eyes?

____

4. What color is Judy's hair?

____

5. Does Judy look like her doll?

____

Name ____________________ 1.RL.1, 1.RL.3, 1.RL.10

Reading Comprehension: Fiction

Read the story. Answer the questions.

Dan and Jill

Jill is Dan's little sister.
She likes to play with his toys.
Dan lets her use his blocks.
They love to share.

1. Who is Jill?

____

2. Who is Dan's sister?

____

3. Who likes to play with Dan's toys?

____

4. What do Jill and Dan play with?

____

5. Does Dan like to play with Jill?

____

6. What do Dan and Jill love to do?

____

Name ______________________________ (1.RL.1, 1.RL.3, 1.RL.10)

Reading Comprehension: Fiction

Read the story. Answer the questions.

Playing Ball

Harry and Matt went outside to play baseball. They played in their backyard. Justin and Dan came to play too. Matt threw the ball to Dan. Dan swung the bat. He missed the ball. Matt threw the ball again. Dan hit the ball hard. It flew over Matt's head. All of the boys yelled, "Oh no!" The ball was heading toward a window.

1. What do you think will happen?
   a. Dan will hit a home run.
   b. Matt will catch the ball.
   c. Justin will throw the ball.
   d. The ball will hit a window.

2. Where does this story take place?
   a. a baseball field
   b. a backyard
   c. a house
   d. a school

3. What happened in the middle of the story?
   a. Harry and Matt went outside to play.
   b. A window broke.
   c. The ball headed toward a window.
   d. Dan hit the ball.

4. Who was the batter?

____

5. Who threw the ball?

____

6. Where did the ball fly?

____

7. What did the boys yell?

____

Name ________________________________ (1.RL.4, 1.RL.10)

Reading Poetry

Read the poem.

Chook, Chook

Chook, chook, chook, chook, chook.
Good morning, Mrs. Hen.
How many chickens have you got?
Madam, I've got ten.
Four of them are yellow,
And four of them are brown,
And two of them are speckled red,
The nicest in the town.

by Anonymous

Answer the questions.

1. In this poem, Mrs. Hen proudly tells about her chicks. Draw the chicks in the picture above just as she describes them.

2. Fill in the graph to show how many chicks she has of each color.

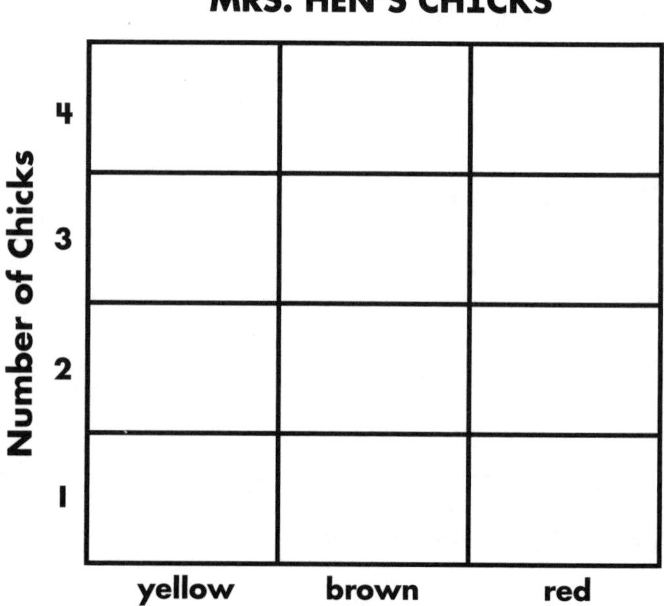

Name ____________________

Reading Poetry

Read the poem.

Trees

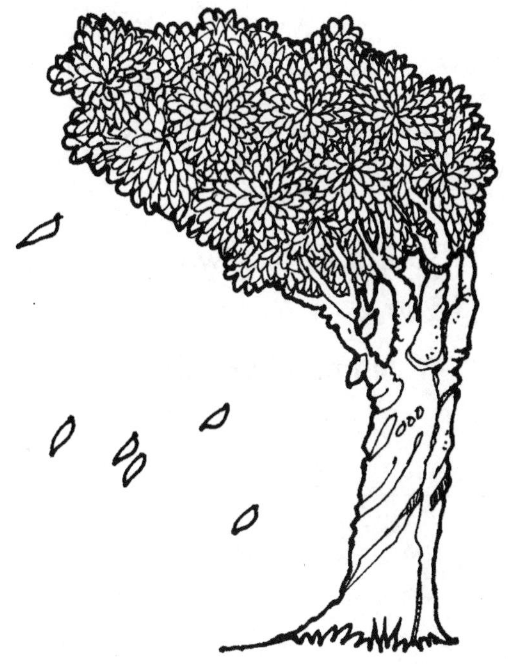

I love trees. They give shade in the summer.

The leaves blow in the wind. Blowing leaves sound like water in a river.

Leaves grow light green in the spring. They turn dark green in the summer. In fall, they turn orange, yellow, and red.

We pick leaves and iron them flat. We hang the leaves in the window all winter.

The snow rests on the tree branches. The snow melts. Tiny buds show up on the branches. I love trees.

Pretend you are a tree. Write about yourself. Use details from the poem.

Example: *I am an apple tree. I love to feel the wind blowing my leaves.*

____

____

____

____

Name ______________________________ (1.RL.4, 1.RL.10)

Reading Poetry

Read the poems.

Wheels

Bikes have two wheels,
Tricycles three.
Scooters have two wheels.
Watch me! Whee!

My Baby Brother

My baby brother rides in his stroller
While I'm on my bike.
We roll down the sidewalk in the sun.
My brother laughs at me riding.
He thinks it's fun
To see his sister smiling
And hear my bell tinkling
And feel my streamers flapping in his face.

Answer the questions.

1. Write two pairs of rhyming words from the poems.

____

2. Write two words that start with the same letter from one line of a poem.

____

3. Which words help you see, hear, and feel what is happening?

____

____

4. Which poem do you like more? Why?

____

Reading Literature

Read the story.

A Day at Wild City

The day was finally here. Ning and Lea were going to Wild City Amusement Park. They had won tickets to the park by reading at school for 500 minutes.

Ning's mom, Mrs. Chan, drove the girls to the park. Mrs. Chan was going to the park too. They all wore matching yellow shirts.

Ning chose the first ride. She chose the Crazy Loop Roller Coaster. It was her favorite ride. Next, Lea chose the Wacky Water Adventure. The girls took turns choosing rides all morning.

In the afternoon, they went to Marvin's Magic Show. They ate pink cotton candy and bubblegum ice cream. Before they went home, they each bought a yellow balloon.

Both girls fell asleep in the car on the way home. They were tired from all the fun.

Number the events from the story in the order they happened.

_______ They went to Marvin's Magic Show.

_______ Ning and Lea fell asleep.

_______ Ning and Lea won tickets to Wild City Amusement Park.

_______ The girls rode the Crazy Loop Roller Coaster.

_______ Mrs. Chan drove Ning and Lea to the amusement park.

_______ The girls bought yellow balloons.

Name ______________________________ 1.RL.1, 1.RL.7

Reading Literature

Look at the pictures. Read the sentences. Draw a line from each picture to the sentences that describe it.

1.

a. Troy plays by a pond. There are ducks swimming in the pond. Many trees grow near the pond.

2.

b. There is a busy street near Carly's house. Many cars drive on the street. There is a bus stop in front of her house.

3.

c. Kristen lives on a farm. A fence is in front of her house. A barn is near her house.

4.

d. Peter lives in a tall building. There is a park near the building. People walk their dogs in the park.

Name ______________________________ 1.RL.1, 1.RL.7, 1.RL.10

Reading Literature

Read the story. Answer the questions.

Drawing

Susan and Carol like to draw. Susan draws pictures of animals. Her favorite animal is a lion. Carol likes to draw people. She draws every day. Susan uses crayons when she draws. Carol uses colored pencils.

1. How are the two girls the same?
   a. They draw animals.
   b. They use crayons.
   c. They draw people.
   d. They like to draw.

2. Which picture did Susan not draw?

a.  b.  c.  d. 

3. Which sentence tells about Carol?
   a. She likes to draw animals.
   b. Her favorite animal is a lion.
   c. She likes to draw people.
   d. She draws with crayons.

4. Think about a good setting for this story. Write a sentence to tell about it.

____

____

Name ____________________ | 1.RL.1, 1.RL.7, 1.RL.10

Reading Literature

Read the story.

The Twins

Kim and Kris are twins. They like to do a lot of the same things. They both like to jump rope, swim, and ride bikes.

But, even twins like to do different things. Kim likes to play baseball while Kris likes to dance. In the winter, Kim likes to ice-skate. Kris likes to go sledding. To help their mother, Kim sets the table. Kris sweeps the floor.

Both girls think it is fun to have a twin.

List three things Kim likes to do and three things Kris likes to do.
Then, list three things both girls like to do.

Kim	Kris
____________	____________
____________	____________
____________	____________

Both

____

____

____

Name ______________________________ (1.RL.9, 1.RL.10)

Compare and Contrast When Reading

Read the story.

Whose Job Is It?

In the plains of Africa, a pride of lions lives together. A beautiful male lion walks around his family. He roars and scares other lions away. The female lions take care of the cubs. They play and stay together.

When a herd of zebras runs nearby, the female lions hunt. The females run fast and catch food for the pride.

The lions work together to keep their home and find food.

Complete the chart. Use the phrases from the Job Bank.

Job Bank

keeps other lions away   hunts

takes care of cubs

WHO DOES EACH JOB?

Male Lion	Female Lion

Name ______________________________ (1.RL.9, 1.RL.10)

Compare and Contrast When Reading

Read the story.

Best Friends

Rita and Maya are best friends. They have the same haircut. They wear the same clothes. They both love to read books.

Both girls have a pet. Rita has a bird. Maya has a mouse. Rita lets her bird Jade fly around her room. Maya keeps her mouse Julius in his cage. Rita and Maya take good care of their pets.

Answer the questions.

1. What do Rita and Maya love to do?

____

2. How do the girls look alike?

____

3. What is different about the girls?

____

4. How do they play differently with their pets?

____

Name ______________________________ (1.RL.9, 1.RL.10)

Compare and Contrast When Reading

Read the story.

Sisters

My big sister loves to talk. She talks about what she sees and does. She reads books when she is not talking. She talks about what she reads. She reads about people, animals, and places. I like to listen to her. I am quiet. I like to close my eyes and see pictures in my head. I can see the things my sister talks about. I like to draw pictures too. My sister likes to look at my pictures. She thinks I am smart. I think she is smart.

1. Use the words and phrases in the Word Bank to fill in the Venn diagram.

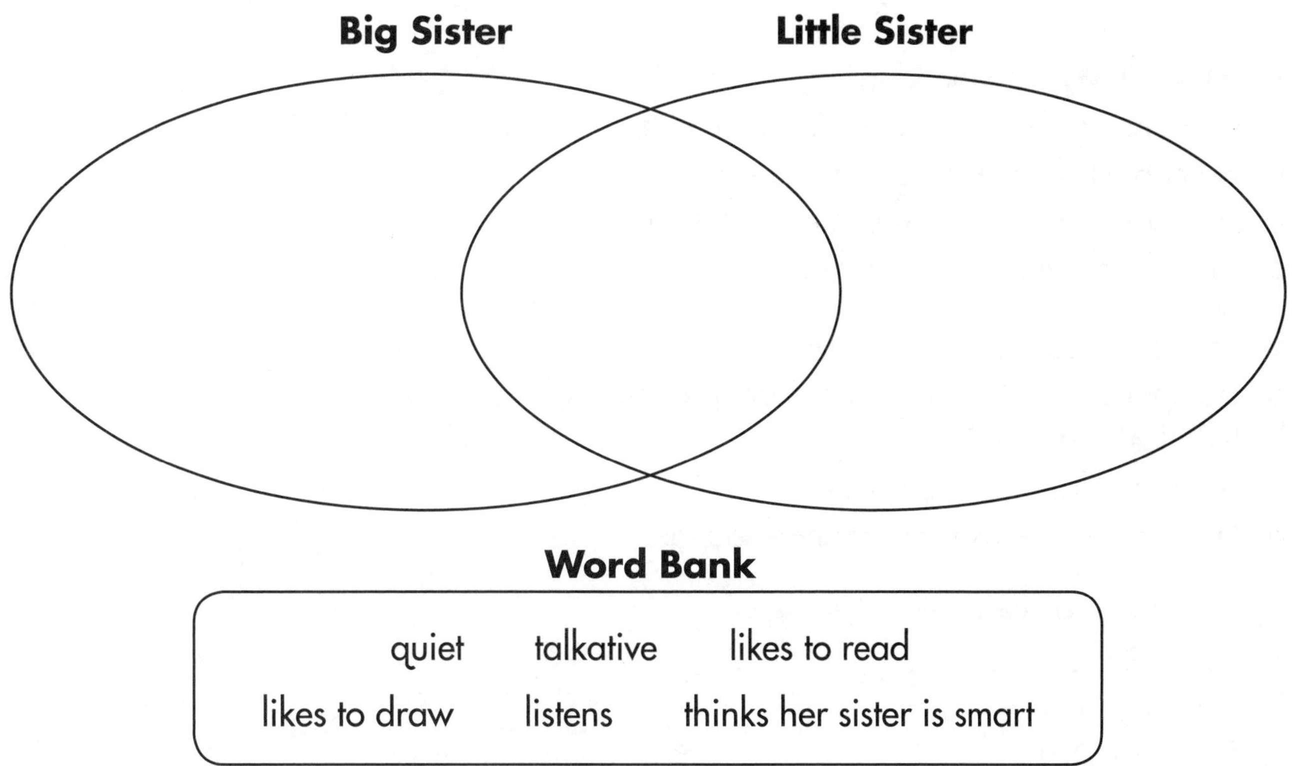

Word Bank

quiet talkative likes to read
likes to draw listens thinks her sister is smart

2. Which sister is more like you?

____

3. What do you like to do best?

____

Name ____________________ 1.RI.1, 1.RI.2, 1.RI.10

Reading Comprehension: Nonfiction

Nonfiction is fact. It is about something real.

Read the story. Answer the questions.

Humpback Whales

One kind of whale is the humpback whale. These whales make very strange sounds. It sounds like they are singing. Their songs can be beautiful. Humpback whales are funny looking. Bumps cover their heads. Like all other whales, they are not fish. They are mammals.

1. What is this story's main idea?
   a. Humpback whales are one kind of whale.
   b. Humpback whales make strange sounds.
   c. Humpback whales have bumps on their heads.
   d. Humpback whales are not fish.

2. What is not a fact from the story?
   a. Humpback whales have bumps on their heads.
   b. Whales are not fish.
   c. All whales are the same size.
   d. Humpback whales make strange sounds.

3. Choose the best title for the pictures.
   a. At the Beach
   b. The Ocean
   c. Small Seashells
   d. Many Seashells

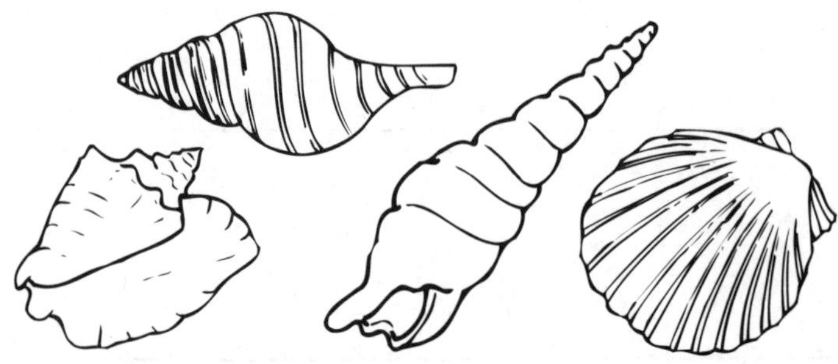

Name ______________________________ (1.RI.1, 1.RI.2, 1.RI.10)

Reading Comprehension: Nonfiction

Nonfiction is fact. It is about something real.

Read the story. Answer the questions.

Tigers

Tigers are very large cats. They live in places like India and China. Tigers are orange with black stripes. They like to eat meat. They have strong jaws and sharp teeth to eat their food. Today, many tigers also live in zoos. You can go see one!

1. What are two places tigers live?

____

2. What do tigers look like?

____

3. What do tigers eat?

____

4. Why do tigers have strong jaws and sharp teeth?

____

5. Where do many tigers live today?

____

Name ______________________________ (1.RI.1, 1.RI.2, 1.RI.10)

Reading Comprehension: Nonfiction

Nonfiction is fact. It is about something real.

Read the story. Answer the questions.

Skunks

Skunks are black and white. They have big, bushy tails. When a skunk is afraid, it makes a bad smell. This smell is hard to wash off. Skunks eat bugs and worms. They also like to eat plants in people's gardens. People do not like this!

1. What colors are skunks?

____

2. What does a skunk's tail look like?

____

3. What happens when a skunk is afraid?

____

4. What do skunks eat?

____

5. Why do some people not like skunks?

____

6. Name another animal you might see in a garden.

____

Name ______________________________ (1.RI.1, 1.RI.2, 1.RI.10)

Reading Comprehension: Nonfiction

Read the story.

Ants

Ants are insects. They have three body parts. Ants also have six legs. They have antennae. Some ants are black and some are red. There are big ants and little ants.

Ants work hard. They work together. Each ant has a different job. Some ants carry sand. Some ants get food. The queen ant has lots of babies. Other ants take care of baby ants. Ants are very strong. They are hard workers.

Complete the sentences.

1. Ants have different

____

2. Some ants carry

____

3. The queen ant has many

____

4. Some ants take care of

____

Name ____________________ (1.RI.1, 1.RI.2, 1.RI.10)

Reading Comprehension: Nonfiction

Read the story. Answer the questions.

Butterflies

Many people like butterflies because they are colorful. Some butterflies may have spots on their wings. They land on flowers and drink from them. Butterflies start out as caterpillars. Caterpillars eat leaves. Later, they grow wings and fly away!

1. Why do many people like butterflies?

____

2. What do some butterflies have on their wings?

____

3. Where do butterflies land?

____

4. How do butterflies start out?

____

5. What do caterpillars eat?

____

Name ______________________________ (1.RI.1, 1.RI.2, 1.RI.10)

Reading Comprehension: Nonfiction

Read the story. Answer the questions.

Pecan Trees

Pecan trees can be found in the southern United States. The trees are tall and have green leaves. Pecans are small brown nuts. You can break open a pecan with your fingers. You can eat the nuts alone or make a pie out of them. Some people like to put pecans on their pancakes!

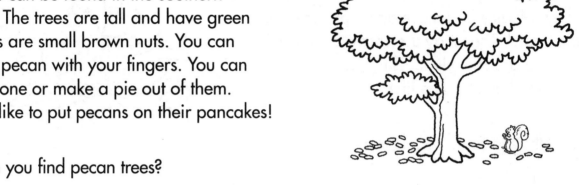

1. Where can you find pecan trees?

____

2. What do pecan trees look like?

____

3. What do pecans look like?

____

4. How can you break open a pecan?

____

5. How do some people like to use pecans?

____

6. Name another kind of nut.

____

Name ______________________

I.RI.1, I.RI.2, I.RI.10

Reading Comprehension: Nonfiction

Read the story. Answer the questions.

Games

Some people like to play board games. They roll dice and move game pieces around the board. They may use cards to tell them what to do. The winner is the person who reaches the finish line first.

1. What do some people like to play?

____

2. What do they roll?

____

3. What do they move around the board?

____

4. What might cards tell them?

____

5. What game do you like to play?

____

Name ______________________________ I.RI.1, I.RI.2, I.RI.10

Reading Comprehension: Nonfiction

Read the story. Answer the questions.

Glass

Many things are made of glass. You can look through a glass window. You can drink from a glass cup. Be very careful! If glass breaks, it can hurt you. Some people use glass to make art. You could make a necklace with glass beads.

1. What are many things made of?

____

2. What can you look through?

____

3. What can you drink from?

____

4. Why should you be careful with glass?

____

5. What could you make with glass beads?

____

6. Name something else that is made from glass.

____

Name ______________________________ 1.RI.1, 1.RI.2, 1.RI.10

Reading Comprehension: Nonfiction

Read the story. Answer the questions.

Dinosaurs

Dinosaurs were big, but they looked and acted like birds. Dinosaurs had hollow bones just like birds do. We all know that birds hatch from eggs. Now, we know that dinosaurs hatched from eggs too. Scientists found some very old nests with eggs that had turned to stone. The nests were far, far apart. A mother that was 23 feet (7m) long could lie on her nest to keep the eggs warm without touching another nest. Dinosaur mothers took care of their babies until they could walk. Bird mothers take care of their babies until they can fly. Scientists think that dinosaurs were just like birds. Maybe birds are just small dinosaurs.

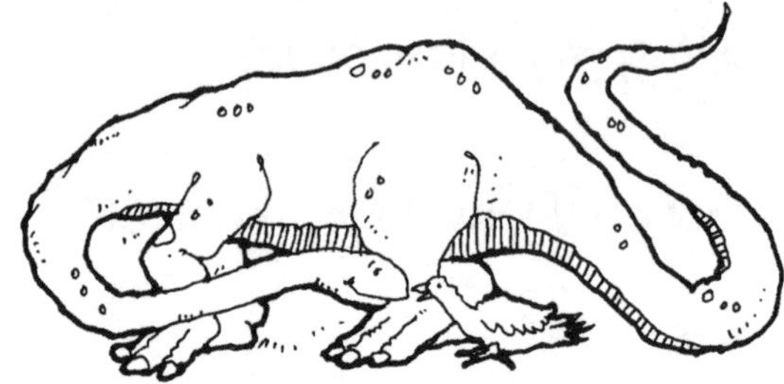

1. What is the main idea of the story?

____

2. List three ways that dinosaurs and birds are alike.

____

____

Unscramble the words to answer the questions.

3. Where did baby dinosaurs come from? **sgeg** ______________

4. What did scientists find to prove this? **stens** ______________

Name ______________________________ (1.RI.5)

Using Text Features

The first page of a book is usually the **title page**. It tells the title of the book, who wrote the book (the author), and who made the pictures (the illustrator).

title → The Magic Sled

by
Jane Brown ← author

illustrator → Illustrated by
Kyle Moore

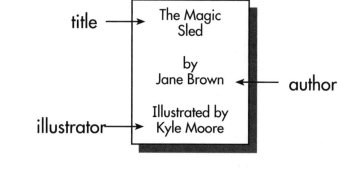

Find two books. Write the title, author, and illustrator of each book on the title pages below.

____
title

by

____

Illustrated by

____

____
title

by

____

Illustrated by

____

Name ___________________________

I.RI.5

Using Text Features

Most chapter books and longer informational books have a **table of contents** after the title page. The **table of contents** tells the beginning page number for the chapters or topics in the book.

Use the table of contents to answer the questions.

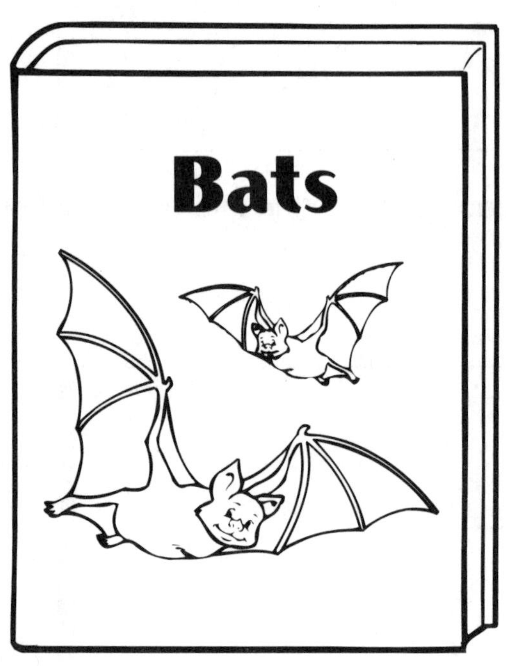

Table of Contents

1. The title of Chapter 2 is ______________________________.
2. Chapter ______________ begins on page 15.
3. How many chapters are in the book? ______________
4. Chapter ______________ would tell you about brown bats.
5. Bats have a thumb on each wing. Chapter ______________ would tell you this fact.
6. Chapter ______________ will tell you what bats eat.
7. Chapter 4 begins on page ______________.

Name ______________________________ (1.RI.5)

Using Text Features

Read the table of contents. Answer the questions.

Bears

1. What chapter tells about how bears act in the zoo? ____________
2. What chapter might tell you how big a baby bear is? ____________
3. On what page does the chapter on grizzly bears start? ____________
4. How many chapters are there? ____________
5. What chapter will tell you how big brown bears are? ____________
6. Could you read about bear food on page 38? ____________
7. On what page does the chapter about bears and people begin? ____________
8. Will this book tell you about a teddy bear that lost a button? Why or why not?

____

Name ______________________

Reading Two Texts

Look at the Venn diagram. Answer the questions.

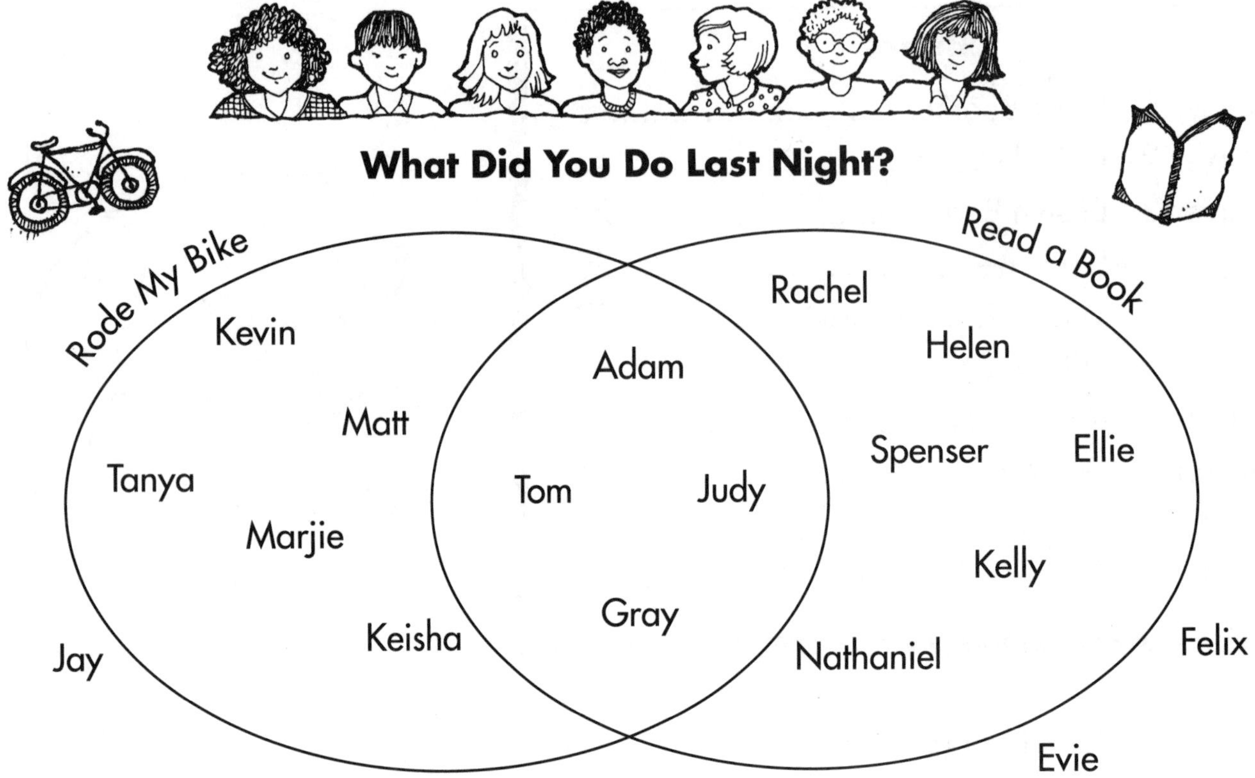

1. How many children read a book last night? ______________

2. How many children did not read a book last night? ______________

3. How many children are in the diagram? ______________

4. Which children did not read or ride their bikes last night?

____

5. How many children rode their bikes? ______________

Name ______________________ (1.RI.9, 1.RI.10)

Reading Two Texts

Read the story.

Alligators and Crocodiles

Is that a log in the water? It doesn't seem to be moving. But, aren't those eyes? Watch out! It's an alligator! Or, is it a crocodile? They look and act very much the same.

Alligators and crocodiles live in the water. They eat fish, turtles, birds, and other animals. Crocodiles have pointed snouts. Alligators have wide, rounded snouts. When an alligator's mouth is closed, you cannot see many of it's teeth. The upper and lower jaws of the crocodile are about the same size. You can see many of crocodile's teeth when its mouth is closed.

Crocodiles and alligators are cold-blooded. This means that both animals stay cool in the water and warm up in the sun. Alligators prefer to be in freshwater. Crocodiles are often found in salt water.

You may think alligators and crocodiles are slow because they lie so still in the water. But, they can move fast on land with their short legs. Both animals are very fierce. Stay away! They may be quietly watching for YOU!

Use the phrases in the Word Bank to fill in the Venn diagram.

Word Bank

eat fish
live in water
pointed snouts
rounded snouts
prefer freshwater
warm up in the sun
stay cool in water
move fast
are fierce

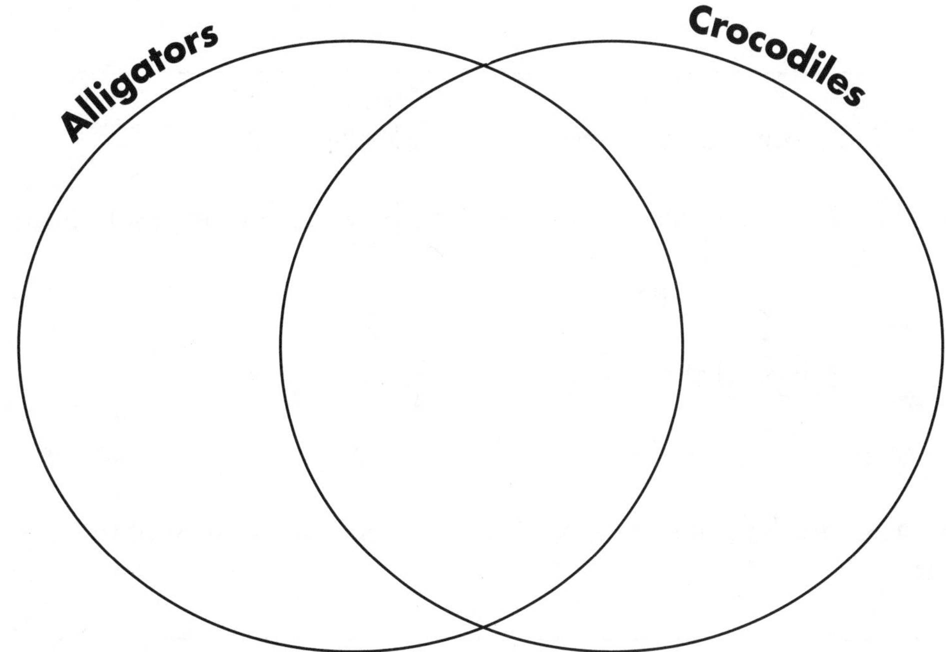

Name ______________________________ 1.RI.9, 1.RI.10

Reading Two Texts

Read the recipes.

Play Dough #1

Ingredients:

1 cup (240 ml) flour
½ cup (120 ml) salt
1 cup (240 ml) water
2 tablespoons (30 ml) cooking oil
2 teaspoons (10 ml) cream of tartar
food coloring

Directions:

Mix the ingredients in a large pot. Cook and stir until a ball forms. Let it cool. Mix the dough with your hands.

Play Dough #2

Ingredients:

1 ¾ cups (410 ml) water
2 ½ cups (590 ml) flour
½ cup (120 ml) salt
2 tablespoons (30 ml) cooking oil
2 tablespoons (30 ml) alum
food coloring

Directions:

Boil the water. Mix with the other ingredients in a bowl. Stir until a ball forms. Let it cool. Mix the dough with your hands.

Circle the best answers. Write the other answers on the lines.

1. Which recipe do you think makes more dough? #1 #2 Why?

____

2. Which play dough needs to be cooked? #1 #2

3. Which ingredient in the second recipe is not in the first recipe?

   alum oil flour

4. Which ingredients are in both recipes?

   alum oil flour salt cream of tartar water food coloring

5. Alum thickens the dough. What do you think cream of tartar does?

____

Name ______________________________ (1.RF.1a, 1.L.2)

Writing Sentences

A **sentence** tells a thought. A sentence starts with an uppercase letter.

Rewrite the sentences. Start each sentence with an uppercase letter.

1. i like studying grammar.

____

2. mary will underline nouns with yellow.

____

3. sandy and Kit underline verbs with blue.

____

4. janice circled the first noun in the sentence.

____

Name ______________________________ 1.RF.1a, 1.L.2

Writing Sentences

A **sentence** tells a thought. A sentence starts with an uppercase letter.

Circle the first letter of each sentence. Write an uppercase letter next to each lowercase letter that needs to be changed.

1. ______ in the afternoon, we learn about science.
2. ______ i get to school at 8:45 am.
3. ______ i sit down at my desk.
4. ______ olivia helps with the calendar.
5. ______ my pencil breaks during math.
6. ______ miss Acker reads a great book.
7. ______ the class eats lunch.
8. ______ we clean out our messy desks.
9. ______ ryan picks me up after school.
10. ______ miss Acker will teach us about volcanoes tomorrow.

Name ________________________________ 1.RF.1a, 1.L.2

Writing Sentences

If the group of words is a sentence, draw an O in the box.
If it is not a sentence, draw an X in the box.

1. ☐ April tossed the ball to Latrell.
2. ☐ Grapes are Lamar's favorite snack.
3. ☐ The scary movie.
4. ☐ Oranges, apples, and bananas.
5. ☐ Dragonflies eat mosquitoes.
6. ☐ Making noise.
7. ☐ The watermelon is juicy.
8. ☐ Andra's baseball bat.
9. ☐ In the spider web.
10. ☐ I am excited to learn about volcanoes.
11. ☐ Clay and red paint.

Name ______________________ (1.RF.1a, 1.L.2)

Writing Sentences

An **interrogative sentence** is called a question. An interrogative sentence always ends with a question mark (?).

Use words in the Word Bank to finish the interrogative sentences. End each sentence with a question mark.

Word Bank

crayons	bag	desk	sneeze
lunch	fit	dot	sticky

1. Is the glue ______________
2. Do elephants ______________
3. Do your new shoes ______________
4. Is an ant as small as a ______________
5. What will you eat for ______________
6. Will you color with the ______________
7. Why are you sitting at my ______________
8. What is in that paper ______________

Name ________________________ 1.RF.1a, 1.L.2

Writing Sentences

Write the correct punctuation mark at the end of each sentence.

1. Where is my pencil ☐

2. Geoffrey likes to use his computer ☐

3. Penguins live in Antarctica ☐

4. Who can help me tie my shoe ☐

5. What color is your bike ☐

6. When is Miguel coming over ☐

7. Carrots are good to eat ☐

8. My family likes to go to the museum ☐

9. Will you help me find my soccer ball ☐

10. My favorite color is purple ☐

Name ______________________________ (1.RF.1a, 1.L.2)

Writing Sentences

Write the correct punctuation mark at the end of each sentence.

1. A tree grows in our backyard ☐
2. Are the leaves on the branches important to the tree ☐
3. The leaves make food for the tree ☐
4. Leaves also store food ☐
5. What do the roots do ☐
6. The roots pull in water and minerals ☐
7. Where do seeds come from ☐
8. Seeds form in the seed pods ☐
9. Do trees have flowers ☐
10. Trees have flowers or cones ☐
11. Where can trees be found ☐
12. Trees grow in many places ☐

Name ____________________

1.RF.2, 1.RF.2c

Consonant Sounds

Every word has a **beginning sound**. It is the first sound the word makes. The consonant letters *b, d, f, h, j, k, l, m, n, p, q, r, t, v,* and *z* each make one sound.

Say the name of each picture. Circle the letter that makes the beginning sound.

1.	2.	3.	4. 25¢
v f k	h d b	v r f	z q k
5.	6.	7.	8.
l x j	n m r	k h r	p r d
9.	10.	11.	12.
t l j	x z p	z s x	h r k
13.	14.	15.	16.
k p b	l f t	n m r	b h d

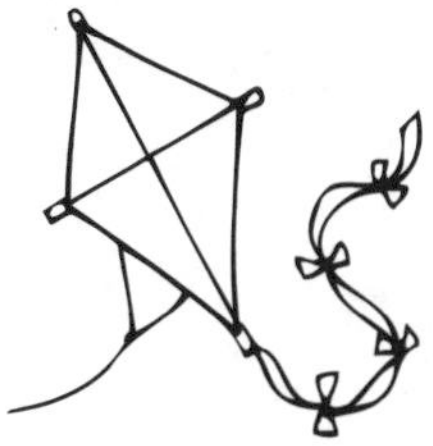

Name ______________________________

1.RF.2, 1.RF.2c

Consonant Sounds

All words have a beginning and an ending sound. The **beginning sound** is the first sound you hear. The **ending sound** is the last sound you hear.

Say the name of each picture. Write the letter that makes the beginning sound.

1.  ______

2.  ______

3.  ______

4.  ______

5.  ______

6.  ______

Say the name of each picture. Write the letter that makes the ending sound.

7.  ______

8. 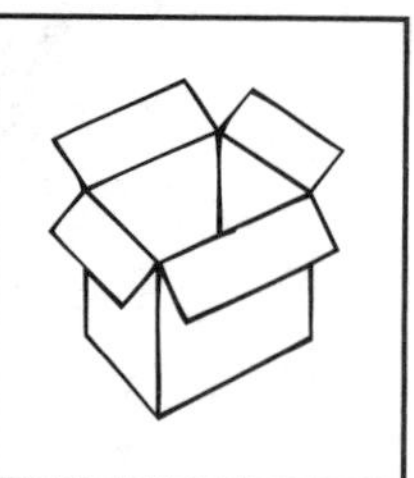 ______

9. 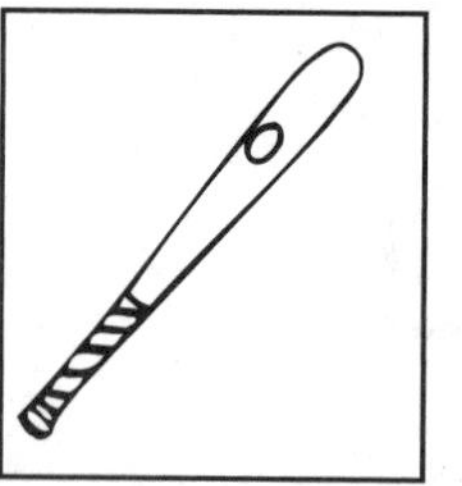 ______

10.  ______

11.  ______

12.  ______

Name ____________________

Consonant Sounds

The **consonants** are all of the letters in the alphabet except *a*, *e*, *i*, *o*, and *u*.

Write the correct word from the Word Bank below each picture.

Word Bank

cow	rose	cent
square	cage	grass
magic	circle	sad

1. 

   ____

2. 

   ____

3. 

   ____

4. 

   ____

5. 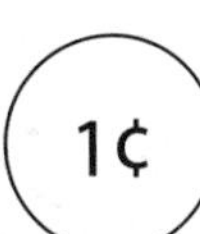

   ____

6. 

   ____

7. 

   ____

8. 

   ____

9. 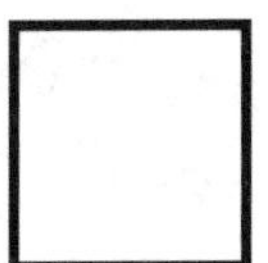

   ____

Name ______________________ 1.RF.3

Rhyming Words

Words that sound alike are called **rhyming words**.
The beginning sounds of the words are usually different.

Write the correct word from the Word Bank below each picture.

Word Bank

boy	shop	brown
two	tent	can
kiss	day	three

1. 

2. 

3. 

4. 

5. 

6. 

7. 

8. 

9. 

Name ______________________________ 1.RF.3

Rhyming Words

Read each list of words. Circle the words that rhyme with the first word.

1. jig	jug	fig	pig	jog	big
2. sap	sip	map	tap	stop	trap
3. vine	fine	tree	line	pine	vet
4. ball	bell	wall	tall	bowl	hall
5. hot	tot	cold	warm	cot	not
6. pail	pill	nail	sail	pile	tail
7. old	young	fold	cold	age	sold

Name ______________________________ (1.RF.3)

Rhyming Words

Read each list of words. Circle the words that rhyme with the first word.

1. glass	pass	gloss	milk	mass	class
2. most	post	toast	tall	bed	host
3. neat	messy	meat	clean	beat	heat
4. tan	can	white	ran	plan	sun
5. stool	chair	cool	pool	sit	fool
6. pen	hen	den	pencil	paper	ten
7. gate	late	slate	door	skate	lock
8. bad	dad	sad	beam	grade	lad

Name ______________________________

I.RF.4, I.RF.4a

Accuracy and Fluency

Read the story.

Robin Hood

Robin Hood lived long ago in England. Robin Hood's king was named Richard. King Richard was away, so the sheriff was in charge. The sheriff was a terrible leader. He made the poor people even poorer. The rich people grew richer.

Robin Hood lived in the woods. He wanted to help the poor people. When the rich people drove through the woods, Robin Hood stole their money. He gave the money to the poor people.

Circle the best answers.

1. Is Robin Hood alive today?

   yes   no

2. Did Robin Hood like the man who was in charge?

   yes   no

3. Who do you think might have been afraid of Robin Hood?

   poor people   rich people   thieves

4. Who do you think probably liked Robin Hood?

   poor people   rich people   thieves

Draw a line to help the rich man get through the woods without running into Robin Hood.

Name ____________________ 1.RF.4, 1.RF.4a

Accuracy and Fluency

Read the story.

Chinese New Year

Chinese New Year is a happy holiday. It comes once a year. Chinese families around the world celebrate. The new year begins in January or February.

There is a colorful parade. The Chinese dragon dances in the parade. The dragon has a colorful head. One person carries the head. Many people carry the dragon's long, long tail. The dragon dances. It tries to catch money from the crowd.

Families get together on Chinese New Year. They set off fireworks. They eat lots of special foods. They eat dumplings. They eat cakes. Some people even eat jellyfish and giant meatballs. Most of all, the families just want to be together.

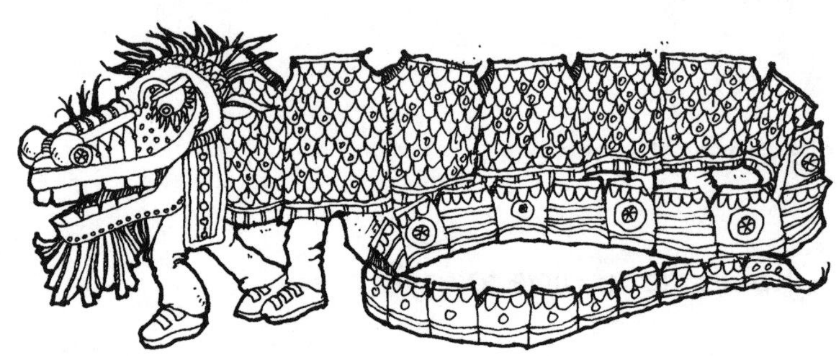

Circle fact or opinion.

1. Chinese New Year is a holiday.	fact	opinion
2. The parade is fun.	fact	opinion
3. The dragon dances in the parade.	fact	opinion
4. The food is wonderful.	fact	opinion
5. The dragon is the best part of the day.	fact	opinion

Name ______________________________ (1.RF.4, 1.RF.4a)

Accuracy and Fluency

Read the story.

Ballet Class

Kira loves ballet class. She goes every Tuesday after school. Class lasts one hour. First, Kira and the other dancers stretch and warm up.

Next, the dancers must warm up their joints at the bar. They bend their legs and bodies. They put their feet in different positions. They hold onto the bar to balance. Kira does some pliés (plee-ayz).

Then, Kira exercises without the bar. She dances in the room with her arms and legs. She is graceful and strong. Dance class is hard work. Her teacher walks around and helps the dancers. He shows Nathan how to hold his head straight. He shows Alice how to relax her shoulders. He teaches them all how to pull in their stomachs.

The next part of class is fun. Kira loves to jump and do pirouettes. They practice special steps and movements. They move with the music.

Kira wants to be a ballerina. She pays attention to her teacher. She knows that being a dancer is hard, but she loves it.

Circle your answers.

1. What does Kira love to do?	paint pictures	dance	ride her bike
2. Which words describe Kira?	fast runner	hard worker	colorful
3. What do you think Kira is like?	good listener	good writer	good babysitter
4. What would Kira say about ballet class?	too long	really fun	very noisy
5. What does Kira want to be when she grows up?	a clown	a dentist	a ballerina

Name ______________________________ (1.RF.4, 1.RF.4a, 1.RF.4b)

Accuracy and Fluency

Write your start time below. Read the story out loud. Then, write the time when you stop reading.

Start Time: ____________

End Time: ____________

How long did it take you to read the story? ____________

Which words were difficult?

____

Read the story.

Skunk Perfume

Why do skunks smell so bad? Well, it's not actually the skunk that smells bad. It's the "perfume" the skunk sprays that smells. That cute little black-and-white animal does not have big teeth or claws to fight off its enemies. The only way to scare away its enemies is with a spray of skunk perfume.

When a big owl comes looking for a meal, the skunk stamps its feet. It puffs up its tail. This does not scare the owl. The skunk is just warning the enemy to stay away. If the warning does not work, the skunk turns around and sprays the owl. This stinky spray stings the owl's eyes. The owl smells this and flies away fast. Wasn't the skunk nice to give a warning first? Next time, the owl will watch out for that cute little black-and-white animal.

Name ______________________________ 1.RF.4, 1.RF.4a, 1.RF.4b

Accuracy and Fluency

Write your start time below. Read the story out loud. Then, write the time when you stop reading.

Start Time: ______________

End Time: ______________

How long did it take you to read the story? ______________

Which words were difficult?

____

Read the story.

Charades

Have you ever played charades? Charades is a fun game to play with a large group of friends. All you need to play is a pencil and paper.

Split the group into two teams. Each team writes down book, movie, and song titles on little pieces of paper. The pieces of paper are then put into two bowls. One person takes a piece of paper from the other team's bowl. That person must act out the title. Her team has to guess what the title is.

First, the player shows the team whether it is a movie, song, or book. The player cannot talk or make sounds. Only hand and body motions are allowed. The player shows how many words are in the title. Then, the team watches the player act out the words. They guess and shout out their answers.

Everyone gets a turn. Both teams play. The winner is the team that guesses the most titles.

Name ______________________________ (1.RI.10, 1.RF.4, 1.RF.4a, 1.RF.4b)

Accuracy and Fluency

Write your start time below. Read the story out loud. Then, write the time when you stop reading.

Start Time: ____________

End Time: ____________

How long did it take you to read the story? ____________

Which words were difficult?

____

Read the story.

The Great Lakes

Stand on the sunny shore of Lake Michigan. Feel the sand between your toes. Hear the seagulls screaming. Look at the water. You can't see the other side of the lake! Is it an ocean? No, it is one of the Great Lakes.

The five Great Lakes are not oceans. Their water is not salty. The Great Lakes are huge freshwater lakes.

Next to the lakes, there are sandy beaches, dunes, rocks, and cities. People play on the beaches, walk on the dunes, and go boating in the water. Many people use the water in their homes for drinking and washing. Others catch and eat the fish in the Great Lakes.

Since the Great Lakes are not salty, there are no sharks or whales. There are many different kinds of fish. There are also ducks, seagulls, and other birds. Seaweed grows in the water.

People must take care of the lakes. They are getting polluted. Trash is on the beaches. Oil is in the water. Chemicals and trash are in the water too. This is bad for the many animals that live in the water. It is bad for the people that live around the water too.

The Great Lakes are beautiful natural resources.

Name ______________________________

1.RL.10, 1.RF.4

Accuracy and Fluency

Write your start time below. Read the story out loud. Then, write the time when you stop reading.

Start Time: ____________

End Time: ____________

How long did it take you to read the story? ____________

Which words were difficult?

____

Read the story.

Magic Trick

"My name is Larry Houdini. Welcome to my magic show! Watch carefully as I make this coin disappear. I reach into my right pocket and take out a handful of coins. Now, I take one quarter from the pile. I'll put the rest of the coins back in my pocket. Now, I will tap my hand with a magic wand. Poof! The quarter is gone!"

Where did it go? Larry is a good magician. Larry can't really make coins disappear. He just makes you look somewhere else. You can do Larry's trick. The trick is that he never took the quarter! You try it. Make sure the back of your right hand faces the audience. Talk to the audience about what you are doing. Make your audience think you took a quarter from your right hand.

Name ______________________________ (1.RF.4, 1.RF.4a, 1.RF.4b)

Accuracy and Fluency

Write your start time below. Read the story out loud. Then, write the time when you stop reading.

Start Time: ____________

End Time: ____________

How long did it take you to read the story? ____________

Which words were difficult?

____

Read the story.

Making Bread

The two main ingredients in bread are flour and water. But, there are other important ingredients too. Yeast is very important. Without yeast, a loaf of bread would be flat. A little sugar or honey is needed to feed the yeast so that it will grow and make the bread fluffy. A little salt adds flavor to the bread. Butter or oil makes the bread tender and moist.

After the ingredients are mixed together, the bread dough is kneaded. To knead, you punch, push, fold, and pinch the dough. Kneading may take 15 minutes. The bread must rest in a warm place for an hour or two so that it can rise. Then, you can shape the bread into loaves. Before it bakes, the bread rises again until it is twice as big as when you started.

When bread is baking, the house smells wonderful. It is hard to wait until it is done!

Name ______________________________ (1.RI.10, 1.RF.4)

Accuracy and Fluency

Write your start time below. Read the story out loud. Then, write the time when you stop reading.

Start Time: ____________

End Time: ____________

How long did it take you to read the story? ____________

Which words were difficult?

____

Read the story.

Yellowstone National Park

Yellowstone National Park bursts with sounds, sights, and smells. Yellowstone is the site of an old volcano. The bubbling hot water and shooting steam are heated from inside the earth. The first people who saw Yellowstone must have thought they were on the moon!

All is quiet. The air is still. Suddenly, water spurts out of the ground high into the air. Old Faithful is a famous geyser in Yellowstone Park. A geyser is a fountain of water that shoots from inside the earth. First, you hear hissing steam. Then, the sound is like 40 showers. After several minutes, the fountain stops. All is quiet again.

The mud pots gurgle and glug. The gray mud bubbles in large, soupy ponds. The ponds smell like rotten eggs. You can feel the steamy heat around them.

Crystal clear pools are as hot as tea. The edge of the water is even with the ground. Sometimes, animals fall into the pools. They don't see them until they are too close. You can see bones in the bottom of some pools.

It is truly amazing to see the wonders of Yellowstone National Park.

Name ______________________________ 1.W.1

Writing an Opinion

Read the story.

Feeding the Dog

Luke has a pet dog named Kip. Luke feeds Kip every morning. He opens the back door and calls Kip. Kip runs to the door. Luke puts food in his bowl. Kip wags his tail and eats.

Answer the questions with complete sentences.

1. Is it hard to take care of a pet?

____

2. Why do you think so?

____

____

3. Write another reason why it might be hard or easy to take care of a pet.

____

____

4. Who do you think enjoys taking care of pets?

____

Name ______________________________ I.W.1

Writing an Opinion

Read the story.

Cooking Soup

Clay is cooking soup. He puts a large pot on the stove. He opens a can of beans. Then, he opens a can of corn. He puts the food in the pot. Clay heats the soup. It will taste great!

Answer the questions with complete sentences.

1. Is it hard to make soup?

____

2. Why do you think so?

____

____

3. Write another reason why it might be hard or easy to make soup.

____

____

4. Who do you think enjoys making soup?

____

5. What foods do you like to make?

____

____

Name ______________________________

Writing an Opinion

Read the story.

Washing Clothes

Ned needs to wash his dirty clothes. First, he sorts the colors. The white shirts go together. He puts the clothes in the washer. Then, he puts in the soap. When the clothes are clean, Ned puts them in the dryer.

Answer the questions with complete sentences.

1. Is it hard to wash clothes? ______________________________

2. Why do you think so?

____

____

3. Write another reason why it might be hard or easy to wash clothes.

____

____

4. Who do you think enjoys washing clothes? ______________________________

5. What other chores can a person do?

____

6. What chores do you like to do? ______________________________

7. What chores do you dislike doing?

____

Name ______________________ (1.W.3)

Writing about Yourself

Read the story.

Playing Tag

My friends and I played tag. We picked teams. Mimi was picked first. She is a good player. Rita ran fast in the game. It was hard to catch her. Then, Zeke hid behind a tree. We could not find him. We were tired at the end of the day. It was a fun day.

Answer the questions with complete sentences.

1. Who plays outdoor games with you?

____

2. When do you play outdoors?

____

3. What game do you like to play together?

____

4. How do you play the game?

____

5. How does the game end?

____

6. What game do you want to play next?

____

Name ____________________ 1.W.3

Writing about Yourself

Read the story.

After School

Erin likes to go to Grandpa's after school. He picks her up at the school gate. They drive to his house. Erin hangs up her coat while Grandpa makes her a snack. She eats the food and then does her homework. Sometimes they watch TV!

Answer the questions with complete sentences.

1. Where do you go after school?

____

2. What do you do first after school?

____

3. What do you do second after school?

____

4. When do you eat dinner?

____

Name ______________________________

Writing about Yourself

Read the story.

Zak's Sister

Zak has a baby sister. He helps take care of her on Saturdays. In the morning, he brushes her hair. In the afternoon, he makes funny faces so that she will laugh. In the evening, he feeds her. Then, he puts her to bed. Finally, Zak goes to bed. Zak's mom says Zak is a good big brother.

Answer the questions with complete sentences.

1. Do you take care of something or someone? ______________________________
2. What do you take care of? ______________________________
3. What do you do first?

____

____

4. What do you do next?

____

____

5. What else do you take care of? ______________________________
6. Why do you take care of this?

____

____

Name ______________________________ (1.W.3)

Writing about Yourself

Read the story.

Our Picnic

Our family went on a picnic in the park. My brother brought a friend. Dad cooked burgers on the grill. I made a salad. Mom served ice cream after we ate. After the ice cream, we played on the swings. Mom and Dad rested under the trees. Then, we went home.

Answer the questions with complete sentences.

1. What would you do to get ready to go on a picnic?

____

2. What would you take to a picnic?

____

3. What would you do at the picnic?

____

4. Where would you play?

____

5. What game would you play first? ______________________________

6. What game would you play next? ______________________________

7. When would you go home?

____

Name ___________________________ (1.W.6, 1.W.8)

Gathering Information

Read the story.

Picking a Puppy

Mom said I could get a pet. We went to the store. We looked at some puppies. A black one licked me. Then, a white one wagged her tail. It was hard to choose. We picked the little spotted puppy with the sad eyes. I will take good care of him.

Answer the questions with complete sentences. Gather information from books and the computer to help you. Share your information with a friend.

1. Where do people get puppies?

____

____

2. Why do people want puppies?

____

____

3. What are two things a new puppy needs?

____

____

Name ______________________________ (1.W.6, 1.W.8)

Gathering Information

Read the story.

Emmy's Hamster

Emmy has a pet hamster. She takes good care of him. Every day she cleans his cage. Then, she feeds him grain and seeds. After that, she puts him on her lap and plays with him. She puts him back in his cage. He runs in a wheel. Emmy thinks hamsters are fun pets!

Answer the questions with complete sentences. Gather information from books and the computer to help you. Share your information with a friend.

1. Where do people get hamsters?

____

____

2. Why do people want hamsters?

____

____

3. What do you need to take care of a hamster?

____

____

4. What are two things hamsters likes to do?

____

____

Name ____________________ I.W.6, I.W.8

Gathering Information

Read the story.

Lightning

The sky lights up with a flash. Crash! Thunder booms. Lightning is a very big electric spark. Thunder is the noise made by lightning.

Lightning happens during a storm. The dark clouds fill with a charge. The electricity in the clouds moves very fast to the ground. The path of the electricity is a bright streak of light. It is called lightning.

Lightning moves faster than its sound. When lightning is close, you hear the thunder at the same time. When lightning is far away, the thunder booms later. When you see lightning, count the seconds until the thunder. If you count five seconds, the lightning is one mile (1.6 km) away. If you count 10 seconds, the lightning is two miles (3.2 km) away.

Answer the questions with complete sentences. Gather information from books and the computer to help you. Share your information with a friend.

1. Why is lightning dangerous?

____

____

2. What are two ways people can stay safe in an electrical storm?

____

____

3. Tell about a thunderstorm you have seen and heard.

____

4. In what season does lightning usually strike?

____

Name ______________________________ 1.L.1e

Choosing Verbs

A **verb** is a word that shows action.

A verb can happen in the past, present, or future.

Read each sentence. Circle the correct verb to complete the sentence.

We **walked** to school. *(past)*

Maya **has** an art class. *(present)*

Jayson **will go** to his grandma's house. *(future)*

1. Ray ____________ well. listen listens

2. She ____________ to play tag. loves love

3. Sheri can ____________ ten laps. swam swim

4. Jen ____________ the circus show yesterday. will watch watched

5. He ____________ the wet shirt and hung it up. dried will dry

Name ______________________ I.L.1e

Present and Past Tense Verbs

A **verb** is a word that shows action.

A verb can happen in the past, present, or future.

Read each sentence. Circle the correct verb to complete the sentence.

1. I like to __________ to the store. walk walked

2. Matt __________ off the high board. jump jumped

3. We want to __________ down the river. row rowed

4. Please __________ your work. finish finished

5. Pete __________ breakfast yesterday. cook cooked

6. We will __________ to play soccer. learn learned

7. Mary __________ down the sidewalk. skip skipped

8. Please __________ to the next chair. move moved

9. My sister __________ to me when I walked by. wave waved

10. We __________ baseball last Saturday. played play

Name ____________________ 1.L.1b, 1.L.1c, 1.L.4c

Noun and Verb Endings

Look at the pictures in each row. Choose the words that go with the picture and write the words in the blank.

one cap

two caps

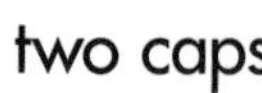

three caps

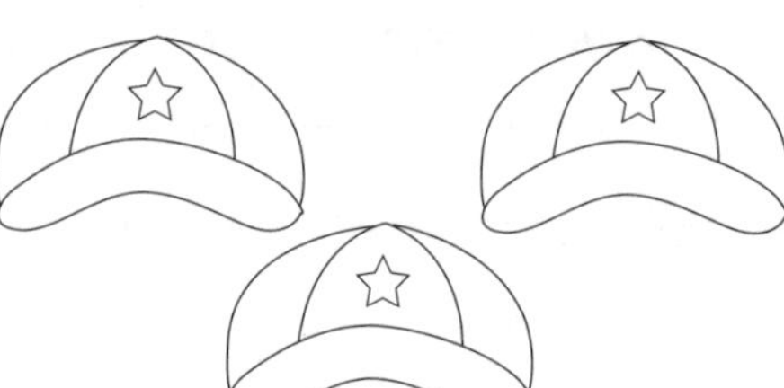

____________________ ____________________

one cat

two cats

three cats

____________________ ____________________

one girl

two girls

three girls

____________________ ____________________

Claudia will ____________ the ball.

Justin ____________ the fish.

catches catch

We ____________ to our teacher.

Uncle Pat ____________ me on the phone.

call calls

Name ______________________ 1.L.1b, 1.L.1c, 1.L.4c

Noun and Verb Endings

Choose the correct word for each sentence. Write the word in the blank.

1. Julie ____________ her dog.

   I ____________ my cat.

   hug hugs

2. They ____________ dinner.

   She ____________ a pizza.

   cook cooks

3. Mom drinks a ____________ of tea.

   The pancakes needed two

   ____________ of flour.

   cup cups

4. Oscar ____________ soup.

   I ____________ salad.

   eat eats

5. We will ____________ fast.

   Lee ____________ home.

   jog jogs

6. The cake ____________ good.

   I can ____________ the soup.

   smell smells

7. Kitty chases all of the ____________.

   Dad gave me a new ____________.

   toy toys

Name ______________________ 1.L.1b, 1.L.1c, 1.L.4c

Noun and Verb Endings

Choose the correct word for each sentence. Write the word in the blank.

1. My ____________ is in a bowl.

   Dad ____________ in the pond.

   fish fishes

2. She ____________ to school.

   They ____________ to work.

   go goes

3. Please get my ____________.

   Mom bought two new ____________.

   watch watches

4. Mom ____________ our team.

   I ____________ my little sister.

   coach coaches

5. I will ____________ the problem.

   Jean ____________ her bike.

   fix fixes

6. Tia rides her ____________ to school.

   I have three ____________ in the garage.

   bike bikes

7. I will ____________ my hair.

   Peg ____________ her hair often.

   brush brushes

8. Sandy visited many ____________.

   I will go to the ____________ tomorrow.

   beach beaches

Name ______________________________ 1.L.1b

Introduction to Nouns

Nouns are words that name people, places, or things.

Which nouns could you find in your desk at school? Draw a line from these nouns to the desk.

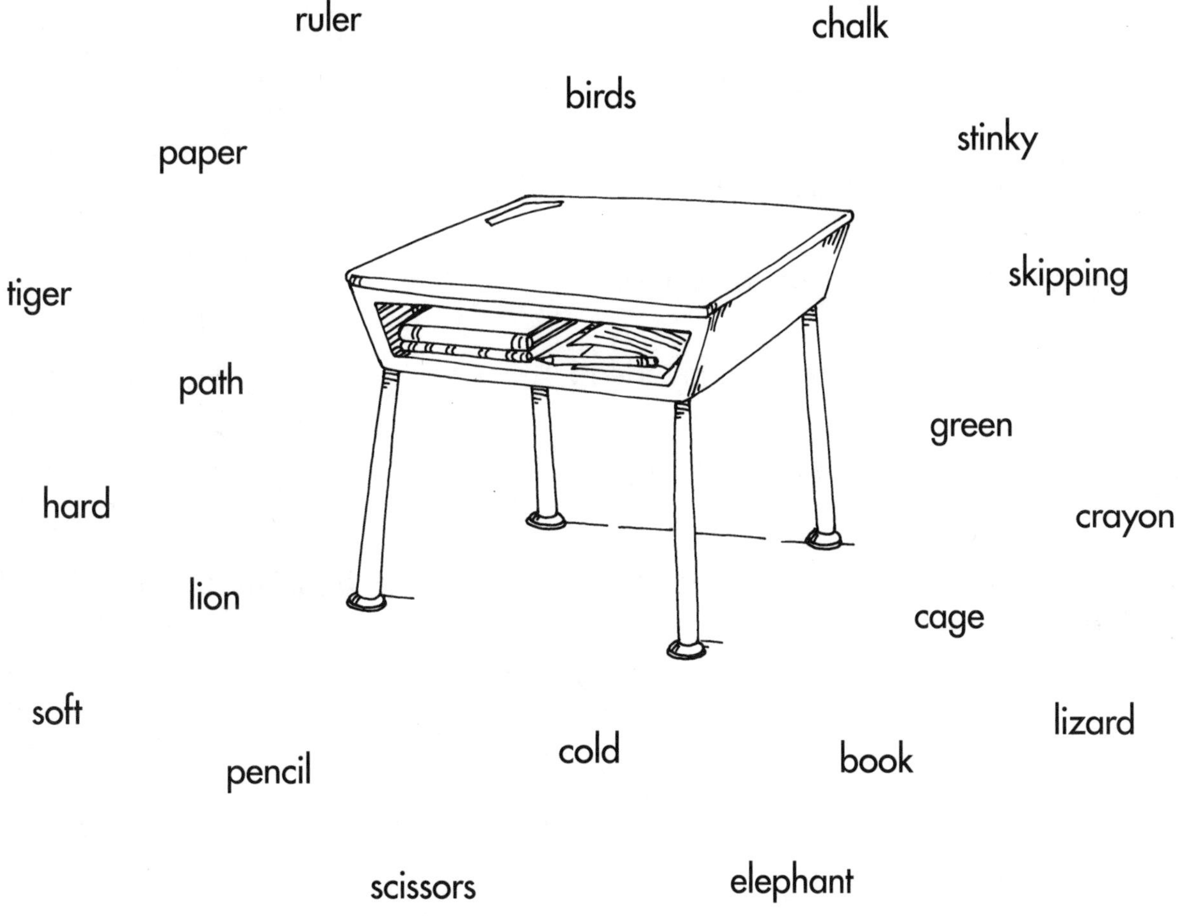

Name ______________________

Introduction to Nouns

Nouns are words that name people, places, or things.

Underline the nouns.

1. Kira has a yellow sun on her shirt.

2. Chase went to the store to buy apples.

3. Her brother watered the plants on the deck.

4. Sabena placed the cupcakes on the counter.

5. The bike on the sidewalk belongs to my friend.

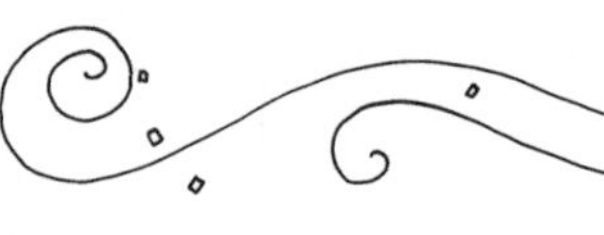

Choose two nouns from the sentences that name things. Draw a picture of each one. Write their names.

6. 

7.

______________________ ______________________

Name ______________________________ (1.L.1b)

Introduction to Nouns

Write each noun in the correct category.

ear	sister	gum
doll	baby	car
Dad	store	playground
Earth	foot	child
doctor	forest	classroom

People	Places	Things
__________	__________	__________
__________	__________	__________
__________	__________	__________
__________	__________	__________
__________	__________	__________

Choose one list from above. Write the nouns in ABC order.

1. __________ 2. __________ 3. __________

4. __________ 5. __________

Name ______________________________ (1.L.1b, 1.L.2a)

Proper Nouns

A person's first and last names are **proper nouns**. Proper nouns name specific people, places, and things. A proper noun always starts with an uppercase letter.

Circle the proper nouns.

Connor Hobart	girl	mom
Maddie Prince	dentist	coach
Ida Alverson	Julio Sanchez	Sandra Olia

Underline the proper nouns in the sentences.

1. Chambers drives race cars.
2. Dylan hiked through the woods.
3. Leon's cat climbed the maple tree.
4. Mikaela King plays the flute at school.
5. Jackson and Nan rode the bus.

Name ______________________________ I.L.Ib, I.L.2a

Proper Nouns

A person's first and last names are **proper nouns**. Proper nouns also include titles, like Mr., Mrs., Miss, Ms., and Dr. A proper noun always starts with an uppercase letter.

Rewrite the sentences correctly.

1. Is ms. smith your teacher?

____

2. cameron kendell sr. is my father.

____

3. Did deidre visit dr. molnar?

____

4. leo marion jr. is leo's full name.

____

5. mr. and mrs. otten are her parents.

____

Name ______________________ I.L.1b, I.L.2a

Proper Nouns

A person's first and last names are **proper nouns**. Proper nouns name specific people, places, and things. A proper noun always starts with an uppercase letter.

Circle the proper noun in each set of words. Rewrite the proper nouns correctly.

1. the park / mullen park ______________________
2. lake huron / a lake ______________________
3. my state / north carolina ______________________
4. new york city / her city ______________________
5. the doctor / dr. beth calhoun ______________________
6. mrs. oltoff / his mother ______________________
7. meg michaels / my friend ______________________
8. my street / transil street ______________________
9. the dentist / dr. wood ______________________
10. king street primary / her school ______________________

Name ____________________________

More Verbs

A **verb** tells what someone or something is doing.

Underline the verb in each sentence. Draw a line from each sentence to the picture it matches.

1. The clown gives balloons to the children.

2. The seals balance balls on their noses.

3. The man sells treats like cotton candy.

Write two sentences about the circus. You must have one verb in each sentence.

4. ____

5. ____

Name ______________________________ (1.L.1, 1.L.1c)

More Verbs

> A **verb** tells what someone or something is doing.
>
> Example: *The boy* ***swings*** *the golf club.*

Underline the verb in each sentence.

1. My sister Emily slides down the slide.
2. My dad pushes Paige on the merry-go-round.
3. My brother Hal climbs the big tree.
4. My grandmother sits on the bench.
5. My grandfather hits the ball with a racket.
6. My mom catches Emily at the bottom.
7. I swing across the monkey bars.

Name ______________________ (1.L.1, 1.L.1c)

More Verbs

A **verb** tells what someone or something is doing.

Choose the correct verb from the Word Bank to finish each sentence.

Word Bank

blew	boomed	burns	drifted	fall
flashed	flowed	floated	shine	soaked

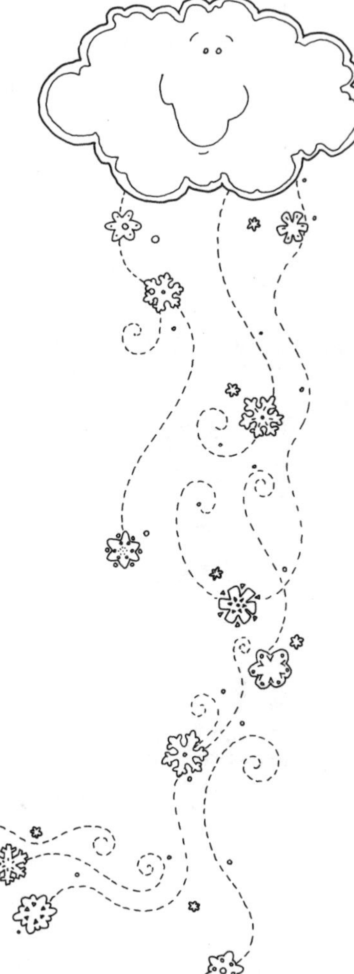

1. The sun ______________ my nose.
2. The thunder ______________.
3. Rain ______________ the sidewalk.
4. Lightning ______________ across the sky.
5. The wind ______________ our kites.
6. The clouds ______________ across the sky.
7. Snowflakes ______________ from the clouds.
8. Many stars ______________ in the night sky.
9. Water ______________ down the gutters.
10. Flurries slowly ______________ from the sky.

Name ______________________________ 1.L.4

Clarifying the Meaning of Words

Sometimes when you are not sure what a word is, use the picture to help you. Look at the picture and say the word for it. Next, look at the written word. Do the sounds from the picture word match the sounds in the written word?

Example: 1. Look at the picture and say the word. 2. Look at the written word. 3. Do the sounds match?

mouse

Circle the word that matches each picture.

1.  desk / dark

2.  flowers / fresh

3.  ship / shoes

4.  treat / teeth

5.  chick / cheese

6. 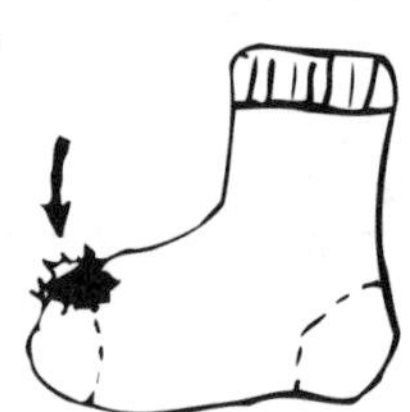 hole / hall

7.  cried / child

8.  tail / tell

9.  bake / break

10.  tree / three

11.  window / winter

12.  chair / share

Name ______________________________ (1.L.4, 1.L.4a)

Clarifying the Meaning of Words

Some words are spelled alike and sound alike but have different meanings. We know which meaning makes sense by reading the rest of the sentence.

Example: *I turned on the **fan**.* *The **fan** cheered.*

Read each pair of sentences. Choose a word from the Word Bank to write on the lines that makes sense in both sentences.

Word Bank

star	saw	fall	roll	back

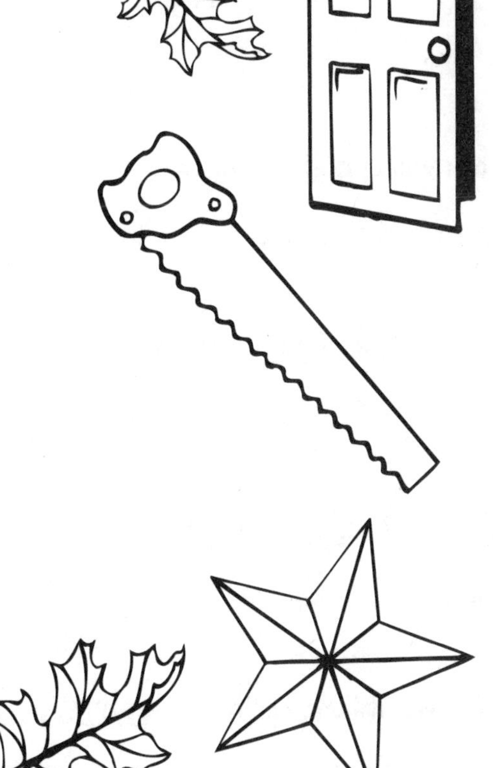

1. Matt ______________ a lion at the zoo.

   Dad cut the tree with a ______________.

2. Leaves change colors in the ______________.

   Raindrops ______________ from the sky.

3. Jan was the ______________ of the show.

   She drew a ______________ on her paper.

4. I ate a ______________ at lunch.

   Sam will ______________ the ball to her.

5. Ann shut the ______________ door.

   Tim swam on his ______________.

Name ____________________ (1.L.4, 1.L.4a)

Clarifying the Meaning of Words

Use clues in each sentence to figure out the meaning of the underlined nonsense word. Circle the meaning of the word.

1. I use <u>xapt</u> to clean.

   fast soap time

2. The <u>zoto</u> hopped in the grass.

   rabbit doll car

3. We planted <u>kibd</u> in the garden.

   ducks boys seeds

4. There is a <u>cefl</u> in the sky.

   door cloud tree

5. We rode our <u>huvot</u> to the park.

   bikes house ball

6. You must <u>japc</u> your room.

   jump sleep clean

7. She went to a birthday <u>leehm</u>.

   party bath plant

8. The cat is <u>niacp</u> the basket.

   sing blow under

Name ______________________________ (1.L.5b)

Categorizing Words

Things can be grouped together because they are alike in some way.

Example:  These could be classified as a group of bugs.

Choose a group name from the Word Bank for each picture. Write it on the line.

Word Bank

pets	shapes	things that go
things to eat	farm animals	tools

1. 

____

2. 

____

3. 

____

4. 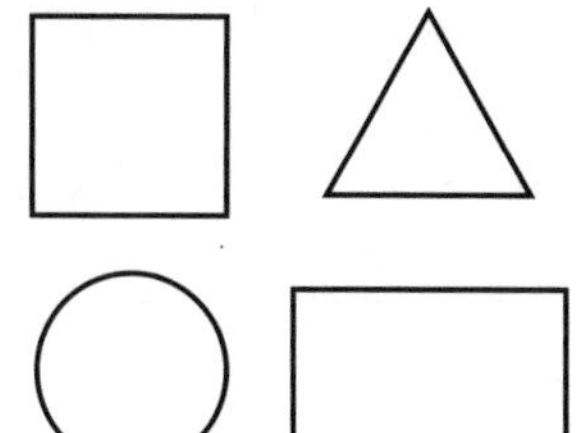

____

5. 

____

6. 

____

Name ____________________ 1.L.5b

Categorizing Words

Read the clues for each riddle. Think about the attributes. Circle the best answer.

1. I am long.
   I have a point.
   I help you write.
   What am I?

   arrow straw

   stick pencil

2. I can fly.
   I have pretty wings.
   I sip from flowers.
   What am I?

   butterfly airplane

   crow bee

3. I am orange.
   I am round.
   I have a green stem.
   What am I?

   pumpkin basketball

   dish sign

4. I climb trees.
   I make funny faces.
   I hang by my tail.
   What am I?

   raccoon bat

   monkey squirrel

5. I have two wheels.
   I can go fast.
   Children can ride me.
   What am I?

   car truck

   bike motorcycle

Name ______________________________ (1.L.2, 1.L.2c)

Commas

A **comma** is a type of punctuation mark used to separate a group of three or more words in a list or series.

Example: *Sal ate* ***grapes, yogurt,*** *and* ***soup*** *for lunch.*

Put commas between the words in each series.

1. Tim went fishing on Wednesday Friday Saturday and Monday.
2. Ahmad Spencer Reese and Jeremy played soccer.
3. Garrett Faith Justin and I drove to the festival.
4. The fair had rides food animals and games.
5. George likes to play with Zack Tommy Cole and me.
6. Antoine's favorite subjects are math reading and science.
7. Perry has relatives in Florida Indiana and Tennessee.

Name ______________________ (1.L.2, 1.L.2c)

Commas

> A **comma** is a type of punctuation mark used to separate a group of three or more words in a list or series.

Circle the commas in the sentences. Answer the questions.

1. We bought bananas, cherry tomatoes, beans, and onions at the market.

2. How many things did we buy? ____________

3. Lynda, Myong, and Joanne made beaded bracelets.

4. How many girls made beaded bracelets? ____________

5. Brady walked, hopped, crawled, and skipped through the obstacle course.

6. How many things did Brady do? ____________

7. Richard saw starfish, eels, clams, fish, and spiny lobsters at the aquarium.

8. How many types of animals did Richard see? ____________

9. Pack your toothbrush, sleeping bag, pillow, and pajamas.

10. How many things should you pack? ____________

Name ______________________________

I.L.1, I.L.2, I.L.2c

Commas

A **comma** is a type of punctuation mark used to separate a group of three or more words in a list or series.

Example: ***Austin, Javier,*** *and* ***Owen*** *went hiking.* (nouns)

Example: *Mia can* ***run, hop,*** *and* ***jump***. (verbs)

Example: *Throw that* ***skinny, little, broken*** *crayon away.* (adjectives)

Circle the commas in the sentences. Write what type of words (nouns, verbs, or adjectives) the commas separate in each sentence.

1. Tyesha, Mario, and Kendall walked away from the beehive.

   ____

2. Molly bikes, hikes, and swims when she goes camping.

   ____

3. We saw anteaters, zebras, jaguars, and bats at the zoo.

   ____

4. I like fresh, hot, salty, buttery popcorn.

   ____

Answer Key

Name ______________________ I.RL.1, I.RL.3, I.RL.10

Reading Comprehension: Fiction

Fiction is a story. It is not real.

Read the story. Answer the questions.

The Zoo

Ms. Soo took her class to the zoo.
The children watched monkeys play.
The monkeys made silly faces.
Then, the monkeys threw popcorn!
The class was sad to go home.

1. Who is Ms. Soo?
   She is a teacher.
2. Where did the class go?
   They went to the zoo.
3. What did the children watch?
   They watched monkeys play.
4. What kind of faces did the monkeys make?
   They made silly faces.

© Carson-Dellosa • CD-104619 5

Name ______________________ I.RL.1, I.RL.3, I.RL.10

Reading Comprehension: Fiction

Fiction is a story. It is not real.

Read the story. Answer the questions.

The Store

Neil likes to shop with his mother.
He pushes the cart for her.
They buy cans of fruit.
They buy cheese and meat.
Neil wants to eat lunch now.
His mother is hungry too!

1. Where does Neil go with his mother?
   Neil goes to the store.
2. How does Neil feel about shopping?
   He likes to shop.
3. Who pushes the cart?
   Neil pushes the cart.
4. What do Neil and his mother buy?
   They buy fruit, cheese, and meat.
5. What does Neil want to do now?
   Neil wants to eat lunch.

6 © Carson-Dellosa • CD-104619

Name ______________________ I.RL.1, I.RL.3, I.RL.10

Reading Comprehension: Fiction

Fiction is a story. It is not real.

Read the story. Answer the questions.

The Fair

Jose and Anita went to the fair. Their parents said they could ride one ride each. Jose rode the Ferris wheel. He pointed at his house from the top. Anita rode the bumper cars. She screamed and laughed when her car hit another one. The fair was fun for both of them!

1. Where did Jose and Anita go?
   They went to the fair.
2. How many rides could each child ride?
   They could ride one ride each.
3. What did Jose ride?
   Jose rode the Ferris wheel.
4. What did Jose point at from the top?
   Jose pointed at his house.
5. Who rode the bumper cars?
   Anita rode them.
6. Why did Anita scream and laugh?
   Her bumper car hit another one.

© Carson-Dellosa • CD-104619 7

Name ______________________ I.RL.1, I.RL.3, I.RL.10

Reading Comprehension: Fiction

Read the story. Answer the questions.

Linda's Tea Party

Linda had a tea party.
Three of her friends came.
The friends were a toy bear, a doll, and a clown.
Linda gave her friends tea and oranges.

1. What did Linda have?
   Linda had a tea party.
2. Who came to the tea party?
   Three of her friends came.
3. Who are Linda's friends?
   The friends were a toy bear, a doll, and a clown.
4. What did Linda give her friends?
   She gave them tea and oranges.
5. Did her friends really drink their tea?
   No, they did not drink it.

8 © Carson-Dellosa • CD-104619

Answer Key

Name ____________________ (1.RL.1, 1.RL.3, 1.RL.10)

Reading Comprehension: Fiction

Read the story. Answer the questions.

Chuck's Sad Day

Chuck was a brown squirrel. His best friend was named Lou. Lou was a black bird. Lou was flying south for the winter. All of the birds were leaving. Chuck was sad. Lou said he would see him again in the spring. They hugged each other.

1. What was Chuck?
   Chuck was a brown squirrel.
2. Who was Lou?
   Lou was a black bird.
3. Where was Lou going?
   He was flying south for the winter.
4. Who was leaving with Lou?
   All of the birds were leaving.
5. How did Chuck feel?
   Chuck was sad.
6. When will the friends see each other again?
   In the spring.

Name ____________________ (1.RL.1, 1.RL.3, 1.RL.10)

Reading Comprehension: Fiction

Read the story. Answer the questions.

Visiting Zuru

Al likes to go to the planet Zuru. His parents came from there. Every summer they return for a visit. They pet the red lions. They eat fruit from blue trees. They swim in the orange sea. Al is sad to go home. He knows he will return soon.

1. Where does Al like to go?
   Al likes to go to Zuru.
2. When does the family visit Zuru?
   They return every summer.
3. What animals does the family pet?
   They pet red lions.
4. What color are the fruit trees?
   The fruit trees are blue.
5. Where does the family swim?
   They swim in the orange sea.
6. How does Al feel when he goes home?
   He is sad.
7. Is this story real or make-believe?
   This story is make-believe.

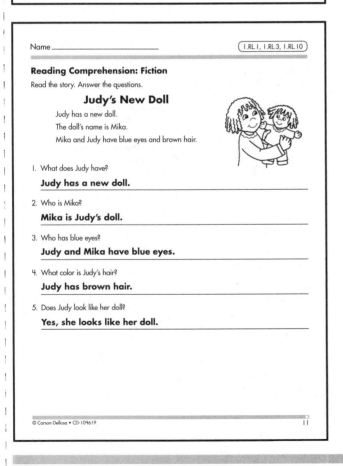

Name ____________________ (1.RL.1, 1.RL.3, 1.RL.10)

Reading Comprehension: Fiction

Read the story. Answer the questions.

Judy's New Doll

Judy has a new doll.
The doll's name is Mika.
Mika and Judy have blue eyes and brown hair.

1. What does Judy have?
   Judy has a new doll.
2. Who is Mika?
   Mika is Judy's doll.
3. Who has blue eyes?
   Judy and Mika have blue eyes.
4. What color is Judy's hair?
   Judy has brown hair.
5. Does Judy look like her doll?
   Yes, she looks like her doll.

Name ____________________ (1.RL.1, 1.RL.3, 1.RL.10)

Reading Comprehension: Fiction

Read the story. Answer the questions.

Dan and Jill

Jill is Dan's little sister.
She likes to play with his toys.
Dan lets her use his blocks.
They love to share.

1. Who is Jill?
   Jill is Dan's little sister.
2. Who is Dan's sister?
   Dan's sister is Jill.
3. Who likes to play with Dan's toys?
   Jill likes to play with Dan's toys.
4. What do Jill and Dan play with?
   They play with blocks.
5. Does Dan like to play with Jill?
   Yes, he likes to play with Jill.
6. What do Dan and Jill love to do?
   They love to share.

Answer Key

Name ____________ (1.RL.1, 1.RL.3, 1.RL.10)

Reading Comprehension: Fiction

Read the story. Answer the questions.

Harry and Matt went outside to play baseball. They played in their backyard. Justin and Dan came to play too. Matt threw the ball to Dan. Dan swung the bat. He missed the ball. Matt threw the ball again. Dan hit the ball hard. It flew over Matt's head. All the boys yelled, "Oh, no!" The ball was heading toward a window.

1. What do you think will happen?
   A. Dan will hit a home run.
   B. Matt will catch the ball.
   C. Justin will throw the ball.
   (D) The ball will hit a window.
2. Where does this story take place?
   A. a baseball field (B) a backyard C. a house D. a school
3. What happened in the middle of the story?
   A. Harry and Matt went outside to play.
   B. A window broke.
   C. The ball head towards a window.
   (D) Dan hit the ball.
4. Who was the batter?
   Dan
5. Who threw the ball?
   Matt
6. Where did the ball fly?
   It flew over Matt's head.
7. What did the boys yell?
   "Oh no!"

© Carson-Dellosa • CD-104619 13

Name ____________ (1.RL.4, 1.RL.10)

Reading Poetry

Read the poem.

Chook, Chook

Chook, chook, chook, chook, chook.
Good morning, Mrs. Hen.
How many chickens have you got?
Madam, I've got ten.
Four of them are yellow,
And four of them are brown,
And two of them are speckled red,
The nicest in the town.
by Anonymous

1. In this poem, Mrs. Hen proudly tells about her chicks. Draw the chicks in the picture above just as she describes them.
2. Fill in the graph to show how many chicks she has of each color.

MRS. HEN'S CHICKS

Number of Chicks	yellow	brown	red
4	filled	filled	
3	filled	filled	
2	filled	filled	filled
1	filled	filled	filled

Color of Chicks

14 © Carson-Dellosa • CD-104619

Name ____________ (1.RL.4, 1.RL.10)

Reading Poetry

Read the poem.

Trees

I love trees. They give shade in the summer.

The leaves blow in the wind. Blowing leaves sound like water in a river.

Leaves grow light green in the spring. They turn dark green in the summer. In fall, they turn orange, yellow, and red.

We pick leaves and iron them flat. We hang the leaves in the window all winter.

The snow rests on the tree branches. The snow melts. Tiny buds show up on the branches. I love trees.

Pretend you are a tree. Write about yourself. Use details from the poem.

Example: *I am an apple tree. I love to feel the wind blowing my leaves.*

Answers will vary.

© Carson-Dellosa • CD-104619 15

Name ____________ (1.RL.4, 1.RL.10)

Reading Poetry

Read the poems.

Wheels

Bikes have two wheels,
Tricycles three.
Scooters have two wheels.
Watch me! Whee!

My Baby Brother

My baby brother rides in his stroller
While I'm on my bike.
We roll down the sidewalk in the sun.
My brother laughs at me riding.
He thinks it's fun
To see his sister smiling
And hear my bell tinkling
And feel my streamers flapping in his face.

Answer the questions.

1. Write two pairs of rhyming words from the poems.
   three/whee, fun/sun
2. Write two words that start with the same letter from one line of a poem.
   Answers will vary.
3. Which words help you see, hear, and feel what is happening?
   Answers will vary but may include whee, roll, laughs, smiling, or tinkling.
4. Which is your favorite poem? Why?
   Answers will vary.

16 © Carson-Dellosa • CD-104619

Answer Key

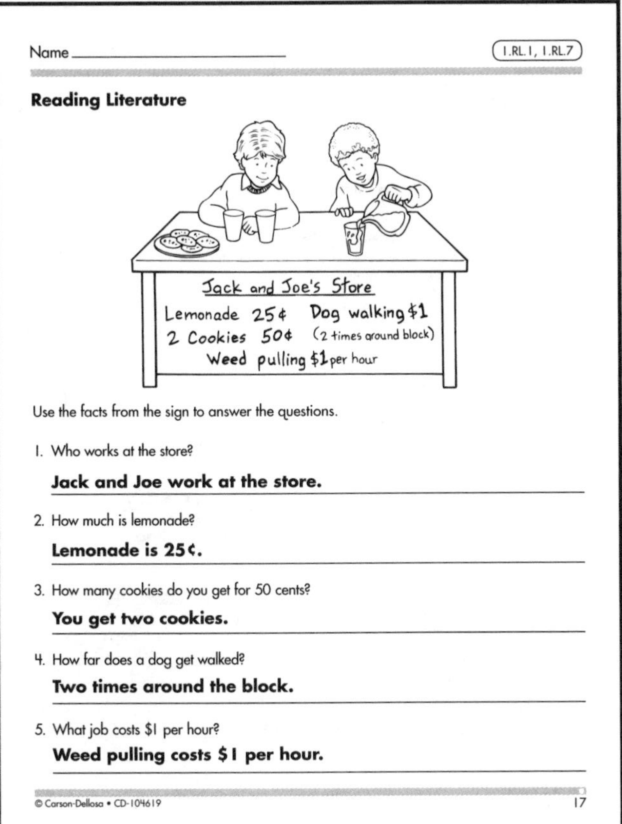

Name ______________ (1.RL.1, 1.RL.7)

Reading Literature

Use the facts from the sign to answer the questions.

1. Who works at the store?
   Jack and Joe work at the store.
2. How much is lemonade?
   Lemonade is 25¢.
3. How many cookies do you get for 50 cents?
   You get two cookies.
4. How far does a dog get walked?
   Two times around the block.
5. What job costs $1 per hour?
   Weed pulling costs $1 per hour.

© Carson-Dellosa • CD-104619 17

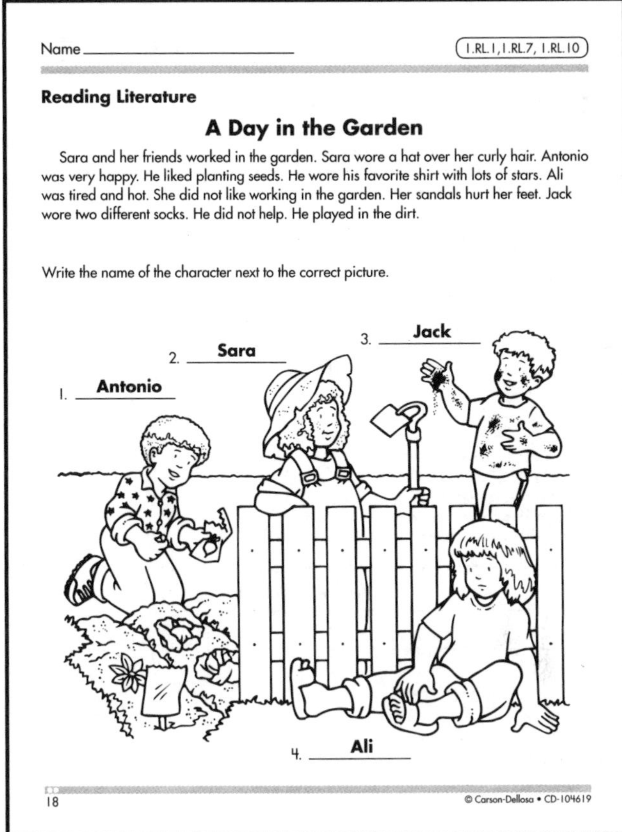

Name ______________ (1.RL.1, 1.RL.7, 1.RL.10)

Reading Literature

A Day in the Garden

Sara and her friends worked in the garden. Sara wore a hat over her curly hair. Antonio was very happy. He liked planting seeds. He wore his favorite shirt with lots of stars. Ali was tired and hot. She did not like working in the garden. Her sandals hurt her feet. Jack wore two different socks. He did not help. He played in the dirt.

Write the name of the character next to the correct picture.

1. **Antonio**
2. **Sara**
3. **Jack**
4. **Ali**

18 © Carson-Dellosa • CD-104619

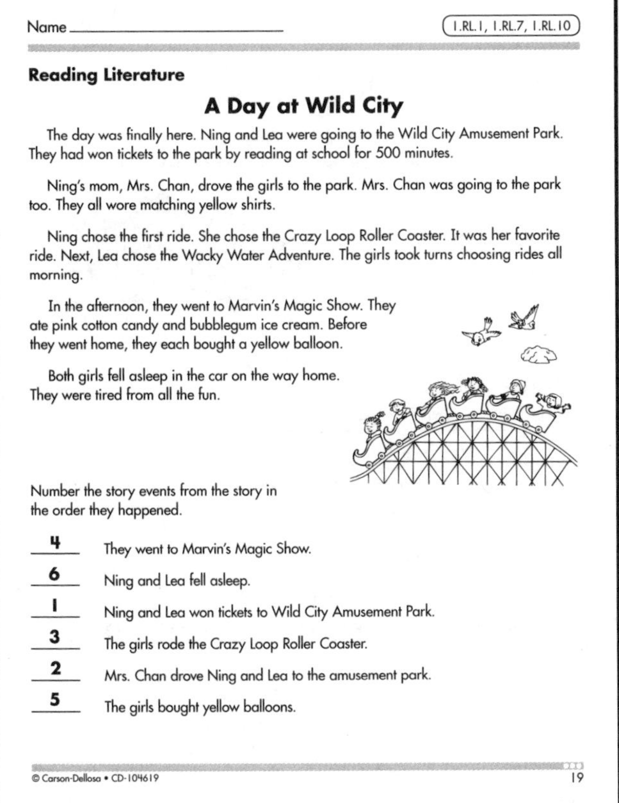

Name ______________ (1.RL.1, 1.RL.7, 1.RL.10)

Reading Literature

A Day at Wild City

The day was finally here. Ning and Lea were going to the Wild City Amusement Park. They had won tickets to the park by reading at school for 500 minutes.

Ning's mom, Mrs. Chan, drove the girls to the park. Mrs. Chan was going to the park too. They all wore matching yellow shirts.

Ning chose the first ride. She chose the Crazy Loop Roller Coaster. It was her favorite ride. Next, Lea chose the Wacky Water Adventure. The girls took turns choosing rides all morning.

In the afternoon, they went to Marvin's Magic Show. They ate pink cotton candy and bubblegum ice cream. Before they went home, they each bought a yellow balloon.

Both girls fell asleep in the car on the way home. They were tired from all the fun.

Number the story events from the story in the order they happened.

4 They went to Marvin's Magic Show.
6 Ning and Lea fell asleep.
1 Ning and Lea won tickets to Wild City Amusement Park.
3 The girls rode the Crazy Loop Roller Coaster.
2 Mrs. Chan drove Ning and Lea to the amusement park.
5 The girls bought yellow balloons.

© Carson-Dellosa • CD-104619 19

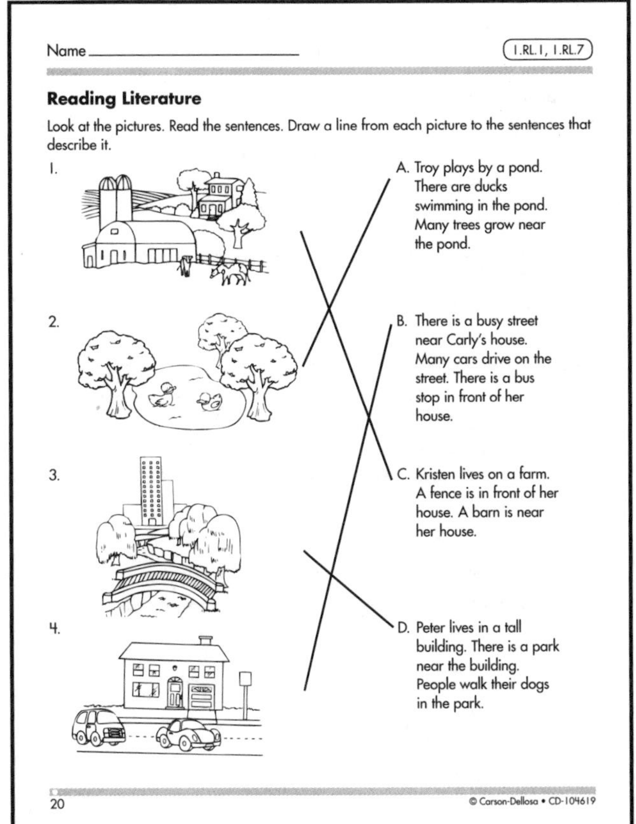

Name ______________ (1.RL.1, 1.RL.7)

Reading Literature

Look at the pictures. Read the sentences. Draw a line from each picture to the sentences that describe it.

1.
2.
3.
4.

A. Troy plays by a pond. There are ducks swimming in the pond. Many trees grow near the pond.

B. There is a busy street near Carly's house. Many cars drive on the street. There is a bus stop in front of her house.

C. Kristen lives on a farm. A fence is in front of her house. A barn is near her house.

D. Peter lives in a tall building. There is a park near the building. People walk their dogs in the park.

20 © Carson-Dellosa • CD-104619

Answer Key

Name____________________ (1.RL.1, 1.RL.7, 1.RL.10)

Reading Literature

Read the story. Answer the questions.

Susan and Carol like to draw. Susan draws pictures of animals. Her favorite animal is a lion. Carol likes to draw people. She draws every day. Susan uses crayons when she draws. Carol uses colored pencils.

1. How are the two girls the same?
   A. They draw animals.
   B. They use crayons.
   C. They draw people.
   (D) They like to draw.
2. Which picture did Susan not draw?
   (A) B. C. D.
3. Which sentence tells about Carol?
   A. She likes to draw animals.
   B. Her favorite animal is a lion.
   (C) She likes to draw people.
   D. She draws with crayons.
4. Think about a good setting for this story. Write a sentence to tell about it.
   Answers will vary.

© Carson-Dellosa • CD-104619 21

Name____________________ (1.RL.1, 1.RL.7, 1.RL.10)

Reading Literature

Read the story.

The Twins

Kim and Kris are twins. They like to do a lot of the same things. They both like to jump rope, swim, and ride bikes.

But, even twins like to do different things. Kim likes to play baseball while Kris likes to dance. In the winter, Kim likes to ice-skate. Kris likes to go sledding. To help their mother, Kim sets the table. Kris sweeps the floor.

Both girls think it is fun to have a twin.

List three things Kim likes to do and three things Kris likes to do. Then, list three things both girls like to do.

Kim	Kris
play baseball	**dance**
set the table	**sweep the floor**
ice-skate	**go sledding**

Both

jump rope

swim

ride bikes

22 © Carson-Dellosa • CD-104619

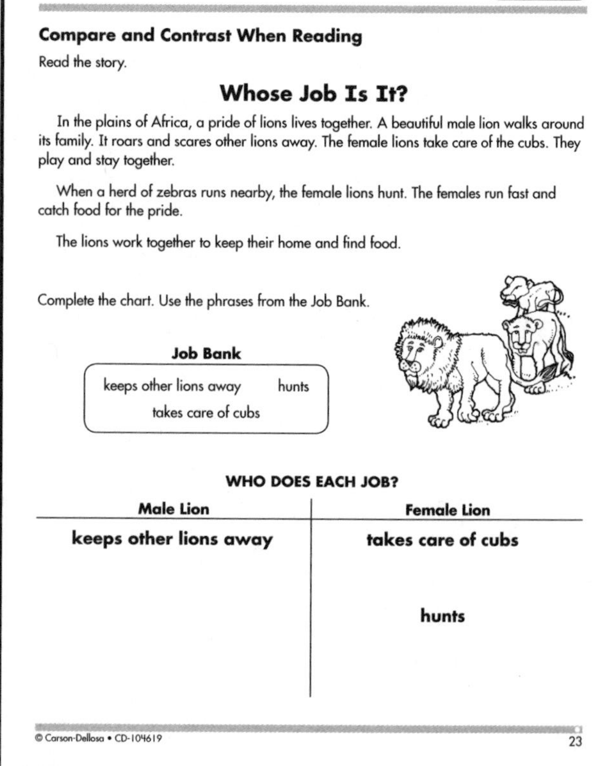

Name____________________ (1.RL.9, 1.RL.10)

Compare and Contrast When Reading

Read the story.

Whose Job Is It?

In the plains of Africa, a pride of lions lives together. A beautiful male lion walks around its family. It roars and scares other lions away. The female lions take care of the cubs. They play and stay together.

When a herd of zebras runs nearby, the female lions hunt. The females run fast and catch food for the pride.

The lions work together to keep their home and find food.

Complete the chart. Use the phrases from the Job Bank.

Job Bank

keeps other lions away hunts
takes care of cubs

WHO DOES EACH JOB?

Male Lion	Female Lion
keeps other lions away	**takes care of cubs**
	hunts

© Carson-Dellosa • CD-104619 23

Name____________________ (1.RL.9, 1.RL.10)

Compare and Contrast When Reading

Read the story.

Best Friends

Rita and Maya are best friends. They have the same haircut. They wear the same clothes. They both love to read books.

Both girls have a pet. Rita has a bird. Maya has a mouse. Rita lets her bird Jade fly around her room. Maya keeps her mouse Julius in his cage. Rita and Maya take good care of their pets.

Answer the questions.

1. What do Rita and Maya love to do?
   They love to read books.
2. How do the girls look alike?
   They have the same haircut and clothes.
3. What is different about the girls?
   They have different pets.
4. How do they play differently with their pets?
   Rita lets her bird fly. Maya keeps her mouse in his cage.

24 © Carson-Dellosa • CD-104619

Answer Key

Name ____________ (1.RL.9, 1.RL.10)

Compare and Contrast When Reading

Read the story.

Sisters

My big sister loves to talk. She talks about what she sees and does. She reads books when she is not talking. She talks about what she reads. She reads about people, animals, and places. I like to listen to her. I am quiet. I like to close my eyes and see pictures in my head. I can see the things my sister talks about. I like to draw pictures too. My sister likes to look at my pictures. She thinks I am smart. I think she is smart.

1. Use the words and phrases in the Word Bank to fill in the Venn diagram.

Big Sister: **talkative**, **likes to read**
Both: **thinks her sister is smart**
Little Sister: **listens**, **quiet**, **likes to draw**

Word Bank

quiet talkative likes to read
likes to draw listens thinks her sister is smart

2. Which sister is more like you?

Answers will vary.

3. What do you like to do best?

Answers will vary.

Name ____________ (1.RI.1, 1.RI.2, 1.RI.10)

Reading Comprehension: Nonfiction

Nonfiction is fact. It is about something real.

Read the story. Answer the questions.

One kind of whale is the humpback whale. These whales make very strange sounds. It sounds like they are singing. Their songs can be beautiful. Humpback whales are funny looking. Bumps cover their heads. Like all other whales, they are not fish. They are mammals.

1. What is the main idea?
   (A) Humpback whales are one kind of whale.
   B. Humpback whales make strange sounds.
   C. Humpback whales have bumps on their heads.
   D. Humpback whales are not fish.
2. What is not a fact from the story?
   A. Humpback whales have bumps on their heads.
   B. Whales are not fish.
   (C) All whales are the same size.
   D. Humpback whales make strange sounds.
3. Choose the best title for the pictures.
   A. At the Beach
   B. The Ocean
   C. Small Seashells
   (D) Many Seashells

Name ____________ (1.RI.1, 1.RI.2, 1.RI.10)

Reading Comprehension: Nonfiction

Nonfiction is fact. It is about something real.

Read the story. Answer the questions.

Tigers

Tigers are very large cats. They live in places like India and China. Tigers are orange with black stripes. They like to eat meat. They have strong jaws and sharp teeth to eat their food. Today, many tigers also live in zoos. You can go see one!

1. What are two places tigers live?

   They live in India and China.
2. What do tigers look like?

   They are orange with black stripes.
3. What do tigers eat?

   Tigers eat meat.
4. Why do tigers have strong jaws and sharp teeth?

   They have strong jaws and sharp teeth to eat their food.
5. Where do many tigers live today?

   Many live in zoos.

Name ____________ (1.RI.1, 1.RI.2, 1.RI.10)

Reading Comprehension: Nonfiction

Nonfiction is fact. It is about something real.

Read the story. Answer the questions.

Skunks

Skunks are black and white. They have big, bushy tails. When a skunk is afraid, it makes a bad smell. This smell is hard to wash off. Skunks eat bugs and worms. They also like to eat plants in people's gardens. People do not like this!

1. What colors are skunks?

   Skunks are black and white.
2. What does a skunk's tail look like?

   The tail is big and bushy.
3. What happens when a skunk is afraid?

   It makes a bad smell.
4. What do skunks eat?

   They eat bugs, worms, and plants.
5. Why do some people not like skunks?

   Answers will vary.
6. Name another animal you might see in a garden.

   Answers will vary.

Answer Key

Name ____________________ (1.RI.1, 1.RI.2, 1.RI.10)

Reading Comprehension: Nonfiction

Read the story.

Ants

Ants are insects. They have three body parts. Ants also have six legs. They have antennae. Some ants are black and some are red. There are big ants and little ants.

Ants work hard. They work together. Each ant has a different job. Some ants carry sand. Some ants get food. The queen ant has lots of babies. Other ants take care of baby ants. Ants are very strong. They are hard workers.

Complete the sentences.

1. Ants have different
   jobs.
2. Some ants carry
   sand.
3. The queen ant has many
   babies.
4. Some ants take care of
   baby ants.

Name ____________________ (1.RI.1, 1.RI.2, 1.RI.10)

Reading Comprehension: Nonfiction

Answer the questions.

Butterflies

Many people like butterflies because they are colorful. Some butterflies may have spots on their wings. They land on flowers and drink from them. Butterflies start out as caterpillars. Caterpillars eat leaves. Later, they grow wings and fly away!

1. Why do many people like butterflies?
   Many people like them because they are colorful.
2. What do some butterflies have on their wings?
   Some have spots.
3. Where do butterflies land?
   They land on flowers.
4. How do butterflies start out?
   They start out as caterpillars.
5. What do caterpillars eat?
   They eat leaves.

Name ____________________ (1.RI.1, 1.RI.2, 1.RI.10)

Reading Comprehension: Nonfiction

Read the story. Answer the questions.

Pecan Trees

Pecan trees can be found in the southern United States. The trees are tall and have green leaves. Pecans are small brown nuts. You can break open a pecan with your fingers. You can eat the nuts alone or make a pie out of them. Some people like to put pecans on their pancakes!

1. Where can you find pecan trees?
   Pecan trees are in the southern United States.
2. What do pecan trees look like?
   They are tall and have green leaves.
3. What do pecans look like?
   They are small and brown.
4. How can you break open a pecan?
   You can use your fingers.
5. How do some people like to use pecans?
   Some people put them in a pie or on pancakes.
6. Name another kind of nut.
   Answers will vary.

Name ____________________ (1.RI.1, 1.RI.2, 1.RI.10)

Reading Comprehension: Nonfiction

Read the story. Answer the questions.

Games

Some people like to play board games. They roll dice and move game pieces around the board. They may use cards to tell them what to do. The winner is the person who reaches the finish line first.

1. What do some people like to play?
   Some people play board games.
2. What do they roll?
   They roll dice.
3. What do they move around the board?
   They move game pieces.
4. What might cards tell them?
   Cards tell them what to do.
5. What game do you like to play?
   Answers will vary.

Answer Key

Name ________________ (1.RI.1, 1.RI.2, 1.RI.10)

Reading Comprehension: Nonfiction

Read the story. Answer the questions.

Glass

Many things are made of glass. You can look through a glass window. You can drink from a glass cup. Be very careful! If glass breaks, it can hurt you. Some people use glass to make art. You could make a necklace with glass beads.

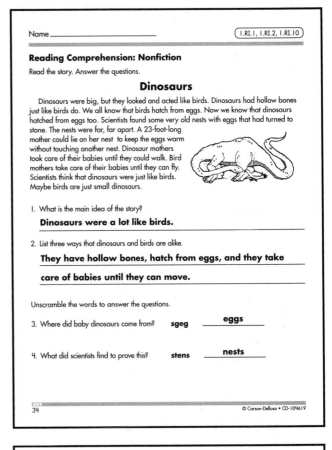

1. What are many things made of?
   Many things are made of glass.
2. What can you look through?
   You can look through a glass window.
3. What can you drink from?
   You can drink from a glass cup.
4. Why should you be careful with glass?
   Glass can hurt you if it breaks.
5. What could you make with glass beads?
   You can make a necklace.
6. Name something else that is made from glass.
   Answers will vary.

© Carson-Dellosa • CD-104619 33

Name ________________ (1.RI.1, 1.RI.2, 1.RI.10)

Reading Comprehension: Nonfiction

Read the story. Answer the questions.

Dinosaurs

Dinosaurs were big, but they looked and acted like birds. Dinosaurs had hollow bones just like birds do. We all know that birds hatch from eggs. Now we know that dinosaurs hatched from eggs too. Scientists found some very old nests with eggs that had turned to stone. The nests were far, far apart. A 23-foot-long mother could lie on her nest to keep the eggs warm without touching another nest. Dinosaur mothers took care of their babies until they could walk. Bird mothers take care of their babies until they can fly. Scientists think that dinosaurs were just like birds. Maybe birds are just small dinosaurs.

1. What is the main idea of the story?
   Dinosaurs were a lot like birds.
2. List three ways that dinosaurs and birds are alike.
   They have hollow bones, hatch from eggs, and they take care of babies until they can move.

Unscramble the words to answer the questions.

3. Where did baby dinosaurs come from? **sgeg** **eggs**
4. What did scientists find to prove this? **stens** **nests**

34 © Carson-Dellosa • CD-104619

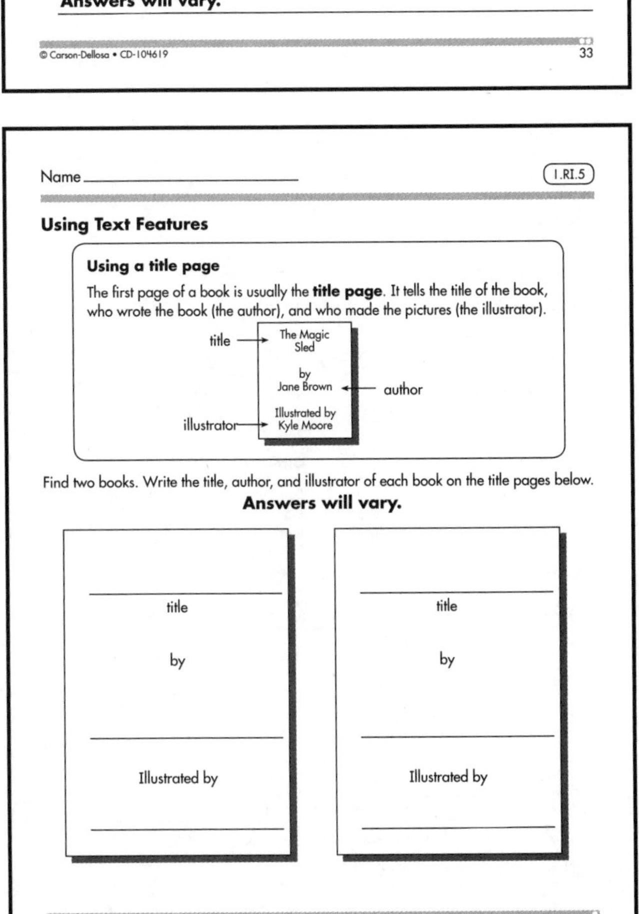

Name ________________ (1.RI.5)

Using Text Features

Using a title page

The first page of a book is usually the **title page**. It tells the title of the book, who wrote the book (the author), and who made the pictures (the illustrator).

Find two books. Write the title, author, and illustrator of each book on the title pages below.

Answers will vary.

© Carson-Dellosa • CD-104619 35

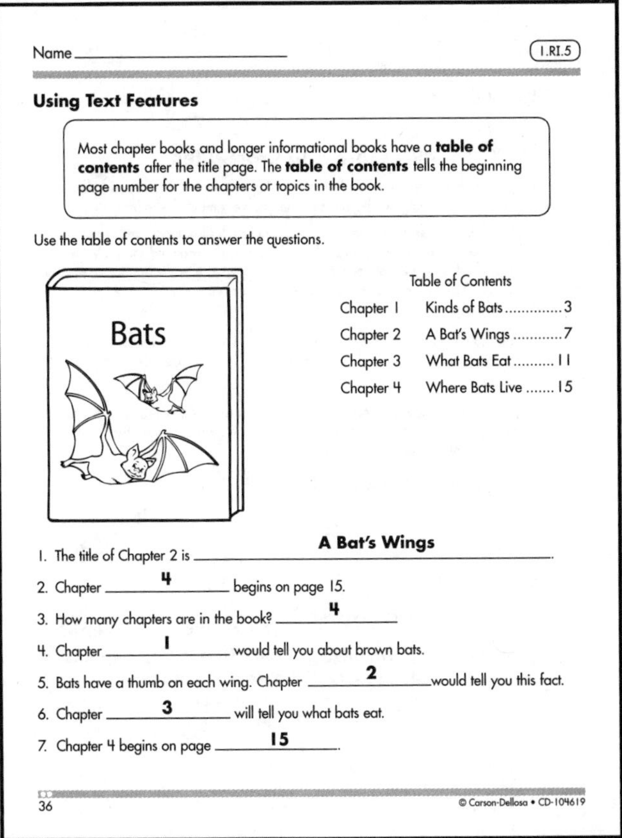

Name ________________ (1.RI.5)

Using Text Features

Most chapter books and longer informational books have a **table of contents** after the title page. The **table of contents** tells the beginning page number for the chapters or topics in the book.

Use the table of contents to answer the questions.

Table of Contents

1. The title of Chapter 2 is **A Bat's Wings**.
2. Chapter **4** begins on page 15.
3. How many chapters are in the book? **4**
4. Chapter **1** would tell you about brown bats.
5. Bats have a thumb on each wing. Chapter **2** would tell you this fact.
6. Chapter **3** will tell you what bats eat.
7. Chapter 4 begins on page **15**.

36 © Carson-Dellosa • CD-104619

Answer Key

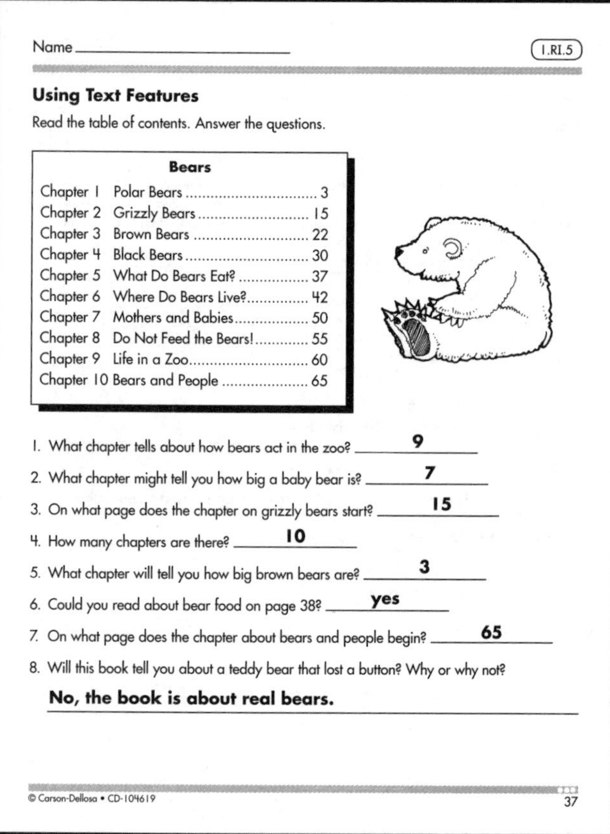

Name ________________ (1.RI.5)

Using Text Features

Read the table of contents. Answer the questions.

Bears

Chapter 1 Polar Bears 3
Chapter 2 Grizzly Bears 15
Chapter 3 Brown Bears 22
Chapter 4 Black Bears 30
Chapter 5 What Do Bears Eat? 37
Chapter 6 Where Do Bears Live? 42
Chapter 7 Mothers and Babies 50
Chapter 8 Do Not Feed the Bears! 55
Chapter 9 Life in a Zoo 60
Chapter 10 Bears and People 65

1. What chapter tells about how bears act in the zoo? **9**
2. What chapter might tell you how big a baby bear is? **7**
3. On what page does the chapter on grizzly bears start? **15**
4. How many chapters are there? **10**
5. What chapter will tell you how big brown bears are? **3**
6. Could you read about bear food on page 38? **yes**
7. On what page does the chapter about bears and people begin? **65**
8. Will this book tell you about a teddy bear that lost a button? Why or why not?

   No, the book is about real bears.

© Carson-Dellosa • CD-104619 37

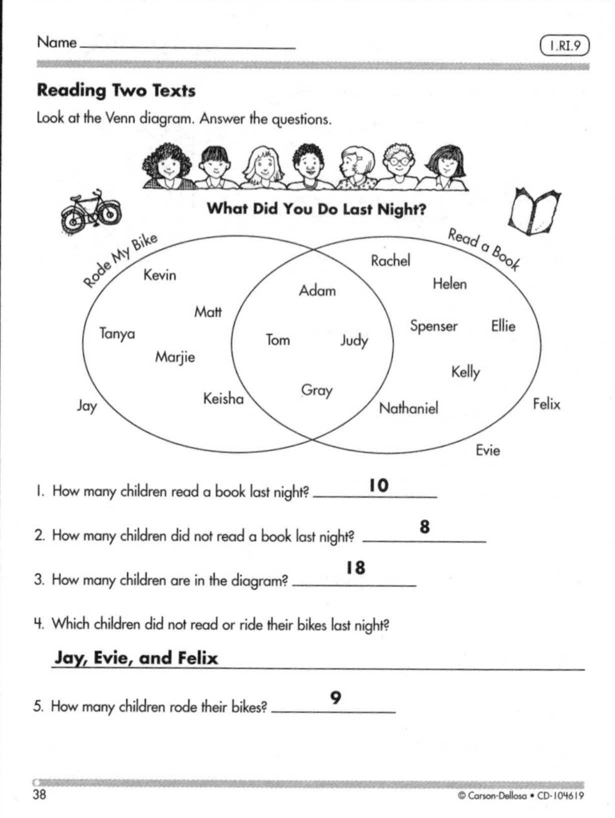

Name ________________ (1.RI.9)

Reading Two Texts

Look at the Venn diagram. Answer the questions.

What Did You Do Last Night?

1. How many children read a book last night? **10**
2. How many children did not read a book last night? **8**
3. How many children are in the diagram? **18**
4. Which children did not read or ride their bikes last night?

   Jay, Evie, and Felix
5. How many children rode their bikes? **9**

38 © Carson-Dellosa • CD-104619

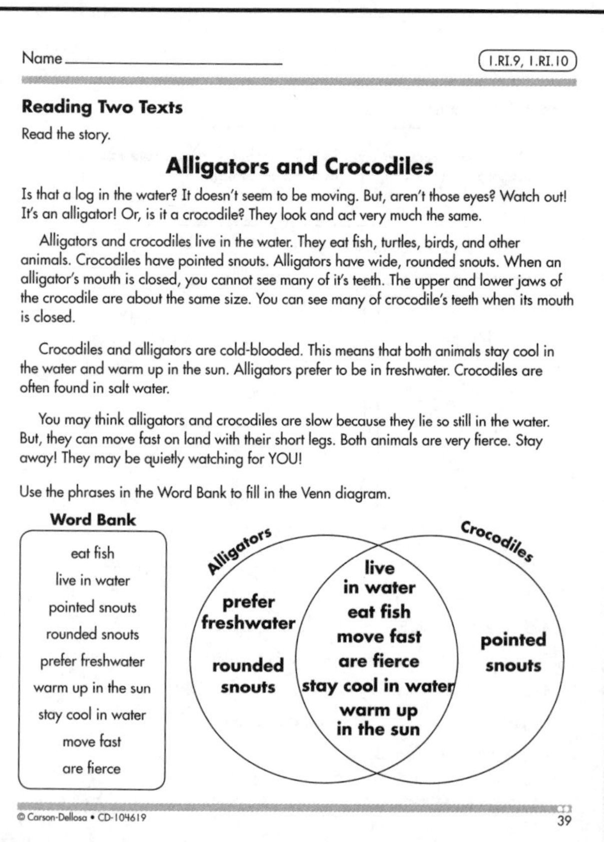

Name ________________ (1.RI.9, 1.RI.10)

Reading Two Texts

Read the story.

Alligators and Crocodiles

Is that a log in the water? It doesn't seem to be moving. But, aren't those eyes? Watch out! It's an alligator! Or, is it a crocodile? They look and act very much the same.

Alligators and crocodiles live in the water. They eat fish, turtles, birds, and other animals. Crocodiles have pointed snouts. Alligators have wide, rounded snouts. When an alligator's mouth is closed, you cannot see many of it's teeth. The upper and lower jaws of the crocodile are about the same size. You can see many of crocodile's teeth when its mouth is closed.

Crocodiles and alligators are cold-blooded. This means that both animals stay cool in the water and warm up in the sun. Alligators prefer to be in freshwater. Crocodiles are often found in salt water.

You may think alligators and crocodiles are slow because they lie so still in the water. But, they can move fast on land with their short legs. Both animals are very fierce. Stay away! They may be quietly watching for YOU!

Use the phrases in the Word Bank to fill in the Venn diagram.

Word Bank

eat fish
live in water
pointed snouts
rounded snouts
prefer freshwater
warm up in the sun
stay cool in water
move fast
are fierce

© Carson-Dellosa • CD-104619 39

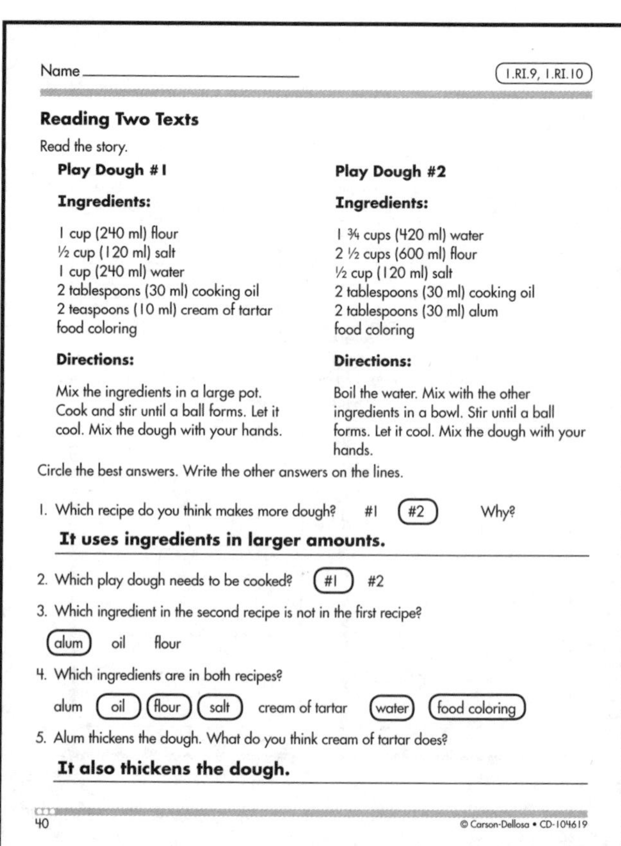

Name ________________ (1.RI.9, 1.RI.10)

Reading Two Texts

Read the story.

Play Dough #1

Ingredients:

1 cup (240 ml) flour
½ cup (120 ml) salt
1 cup (240 ml) water
2 tablespoons (30 ml) cooking oil
2 teaspoons (10 ml) cream of tartar
food coloring

Directions:

Mix the ingredients in a large pot. Cook and stir until a ball forms. Let it cool. Mix the dough with your hands.

Play Dough #2

Ingredients:

1 ¾ cups (420 ml) water
2 ½ cups (600 ml) flour
½ cup (120 ml) salt
2 tablespoons (30 ml) cooking oil
2 tablespoons (30 ml) alum
food coloring

Directions:

Boil the water. Mix with the other ingredients in a bowl. Stir until a ball forms. Let it cool. Mix the dough with your hands.

Circle the best answers. Write the other answers on the lines.

1. Which recipe do you think makes more dough? #1 (#2) Why?

   It uses ingredients in larger amounts.
2. Which play dough needs to be cooked? (#1) #2
3. Which ingredient in the second recipe is not in the first recipe?

   (alum) oil flour
4. Which ingredients are in both recipes?

   alum (oil) (flour) (salt) cream of tartar (water) (food coloring)
5. Alum thickens the dough. What do you think cream of tartar does?

   It also thickens the dough.

40 © Carson-Dellosa • CD-104619

Answer Key

Name ______________________ (1.RF.1a, 1.L.2)

Writing Sentences

A **sentence** tells a thought. A sentence starts with an uppercase letter.

Rewrite the sentences. Start each sentence with an uppercase letter.

1. i like studying grammar.

   I like studying grammar.

2. mary will underline nouns with yellow.

   Mary will underline nouns with yellow.

3. sandy and Kit underline verbs with blue.

   Sandy and Kit underline verbs with blue.

4. janice circled the first noun in the sentence.

   Janice circled the first noun in the sentence.

© Carson-Dellosa • CD-104619 41

Name ______________________ (1.RF.1a, 1.L.2)

Writing Sentences

A **sentence** tells a thought. A sentence starts with an uppercase letter.

Circle the first letter of each sentence. Write an uppercase letter next to each lowercase letter that needs to be changed.

1. **I** in the afternoon, we learn about science.
2. **I** i get to school at 8:45 am.
3. **I** i sit down at my desk.
4. **O** olivia helps with the calendar.
5. **M** my pencil breaks during math.
6. **M** miss Acker reads a great book.
7. **T** the class eats lunch.
8. **W** we clean out our messy desks.
9. **R** ryan picks me up after school.
10. **M** miss Acker will teach us about volcanoes tomorrow.

42 © Carson-Dellosa • CD-104619

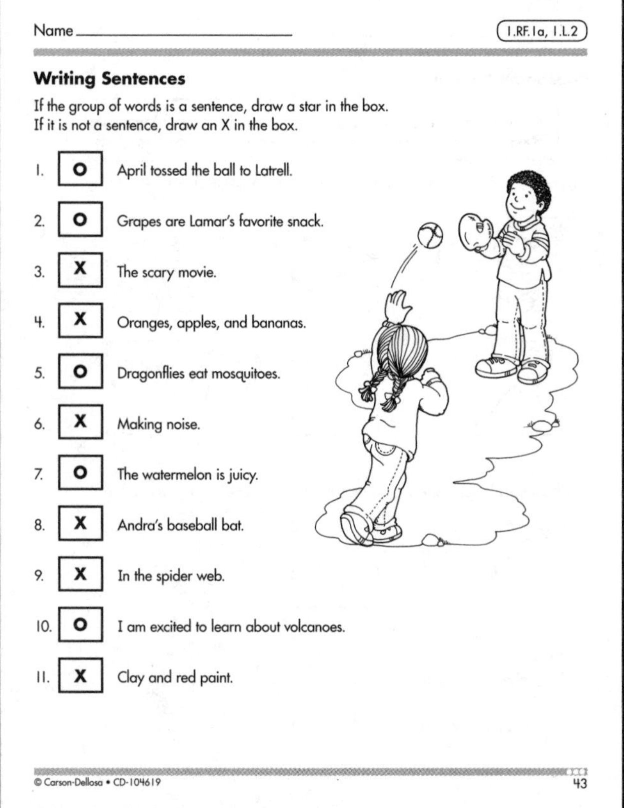

Name ______________________ (1.RF.1a, 1.L.2)

Writing Sentences

If the group of words is a sentence, draw a star in the box.
If it is not a sentence, draw an X in the box.

1. **O** April tossed the ball to Latrell.
2. **O** Grapes are Lamar's favorite snack.
3. **X** The scary movie.
4. **X** Oranges, apples, and bananas.
5. **O** Dragonflies eat mosquitoes.
6. **X** Making noise.
7. **O** The watermelon is juicy.
8. **X** Andra's baseball bat.
9. **X** In the spider web.
10. **O** I am excited to learn about volcanoes.
11. **X** Clay and red paint.

© Carson-Dellosa • CD-104619 43

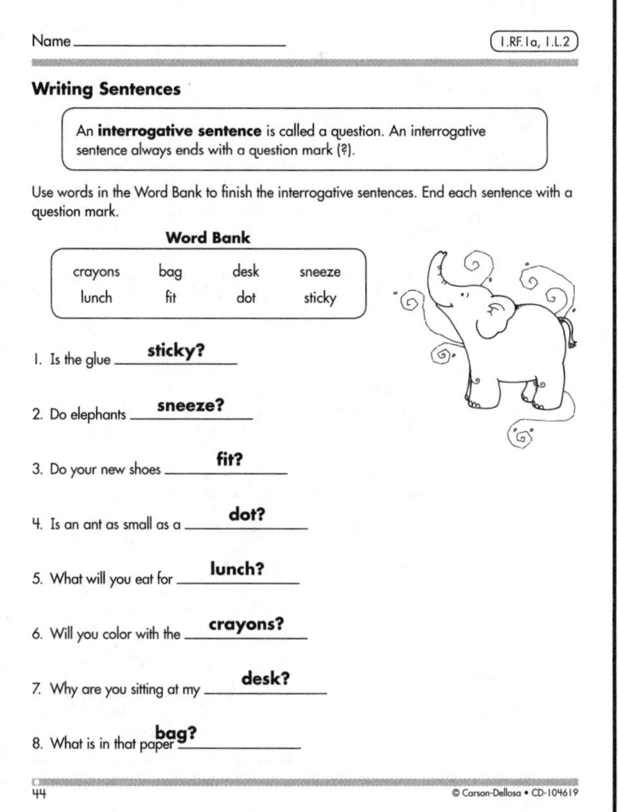

Name ______________________ (1.RF.1a, 1.L.2)

Writing Sentences

An **interrogative sentence** is called a question. An interrogative sentence always ends with a question mark (?).

Use words in the Word Bank to finish the interrogative sentences. End each sentence with a question mark.

Word Bank

crayons	bag	desk	sneeze
lunch	fit	dot	sticky

1. Is the glue **sticky?**
2. Do elephants **sneeze?**
3. Do your new shoes **fit?**
4. Is an ant as small as a **dot?**
5. What will you eat for **lunch?**
6. Will you color with the **crayons?**
7. Why are you sitting at my **desk?**
8. What is in that paper **bag?**

44 © Carson-Dellosa • CD-104619

Answer Key

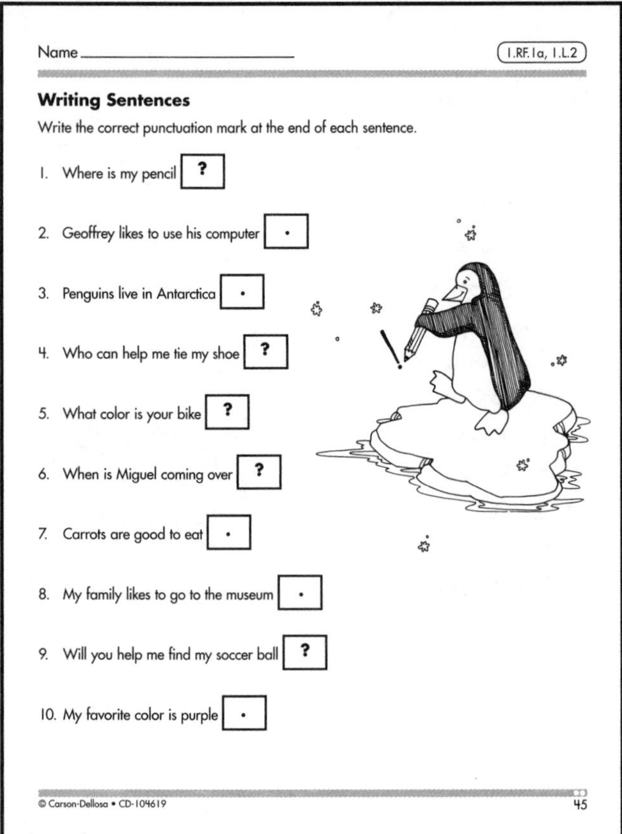

Name ____________________ (1.RF.1a, 1.L.2)

Writing Sentences

Write the correct punctuation mark at the end of each sentence.

1. Where is my pencil **?**
2. Geoffrey likes to use his computer **.**
3. Penguins live in Antarctica **.**
4. Who can help me tie my shoe **?**
5. What color is your bike **?**
6. When is Miguel coming over **?**
7. Carrots are good to eat **.**
8. My family likes to go to the museum **.**
9. Will you help me find my soccer ball **?**
10. My favorite color is purple **.**

© Carson-Dellosa • CD-104619 45

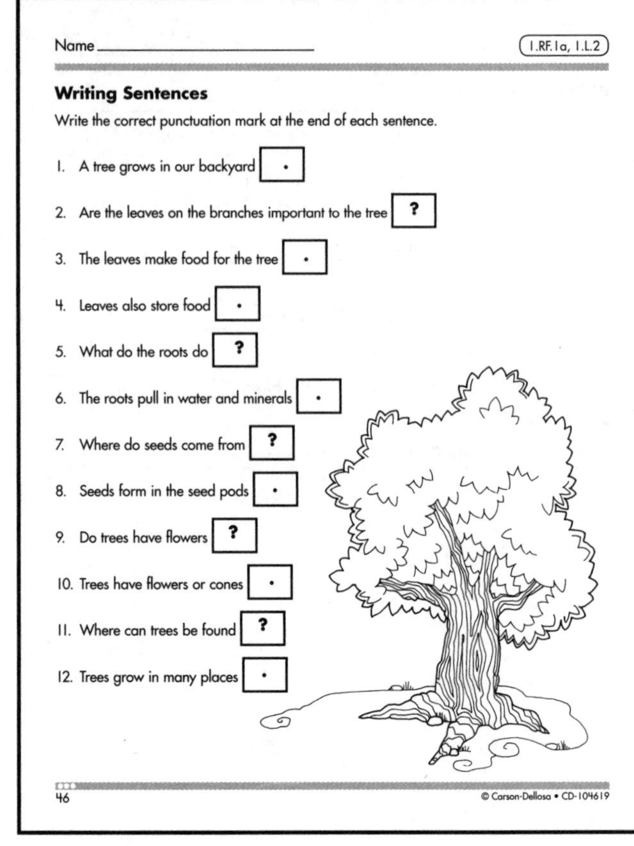

Name ____________________ (1.RF.1a, 1.L.2)

Writing Sentences

Write the correct punctuation mark at the end of each sentence.

1. A tree grows in our backyard **.**
2. Are the leaves on the branches important to the tree **?**
3. The leaves make food for the tree **.**
4. Leaves also store food **.**
5. What do the roots do **?**
6. The roots pull in water and minerals **.**
7. Where do seeds come from **?**
8. Seeds form in the seed pods **.**
9. Do trees have flowers **?**
10. Trees have flowers or cones **.**
11. Where can trees be found **?**
12. Trees grow in many places **.**

46 © Carson-Dellosa • CD-104619

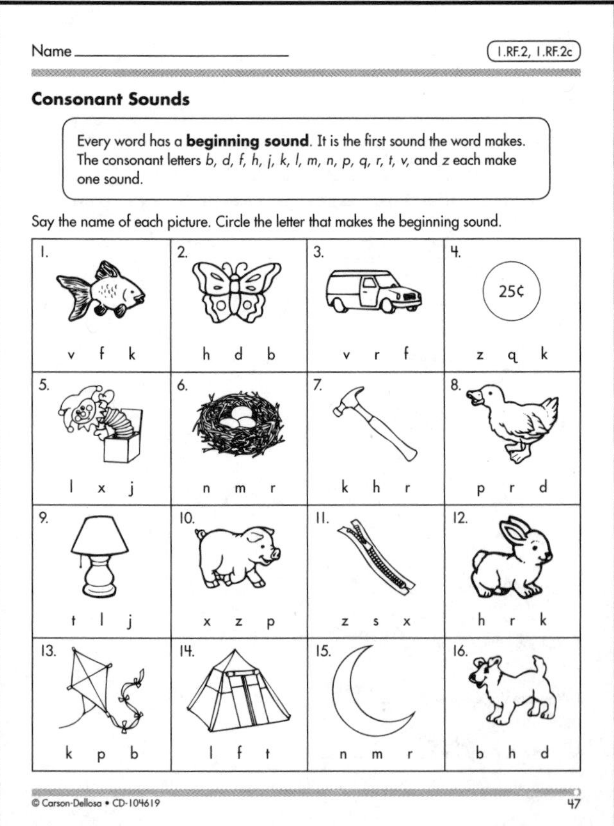

Name ____________________ (1.RF.2, 1.RF.2c)

Consonant Sounds

Every word has a **beginning sound**. It is the first sound the word makes. The consonant letters *b, d, f, h, j, k, l, m, n, p, q, r, t, v,* and *z* each make one sound.

Say the name of each picture. Circle the letter that makes the beginning sound.

1. v f k	2. h d b	3. v r f	4. 25¢ z q k
5. l x j	6. n m r	7. k h r	8. p r d
9. t l j	10. x z p	11. z s x	12. h r k
13. k p b	14. l f t	15. n m r	16. b h d

© Carson-Dellosa • CD-104619 47

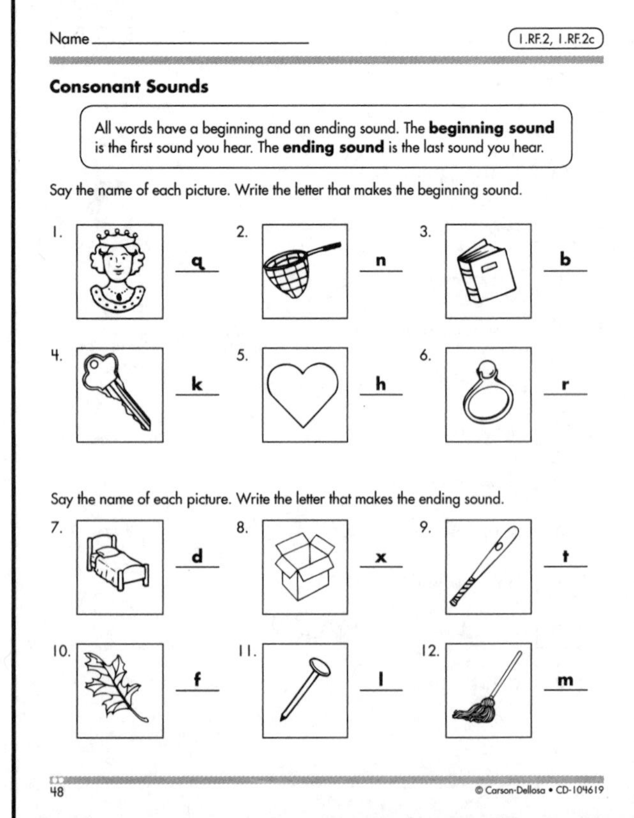

Name ____________________ (1.RF.2, 1.RF.2c)

Consonant Sounds

All words have a beginning and an ending sound. The **beginning sound** is the first sound you hear. The **ending sound** is the last sound you hear.

Say the name of each picture. Write the letter that makes the beginning sound.

1. **q**
2. **n**
3. **b**
4. **k**
5. **h**
6. **r**

Say the name of each picture. Write the letter that makes the ending sound.

7. **d**
8. **x**
9. **t**
10. **f**
11. **l**
12. **m**

48 © Carson-Dellosa • CD-104619

Answer Key

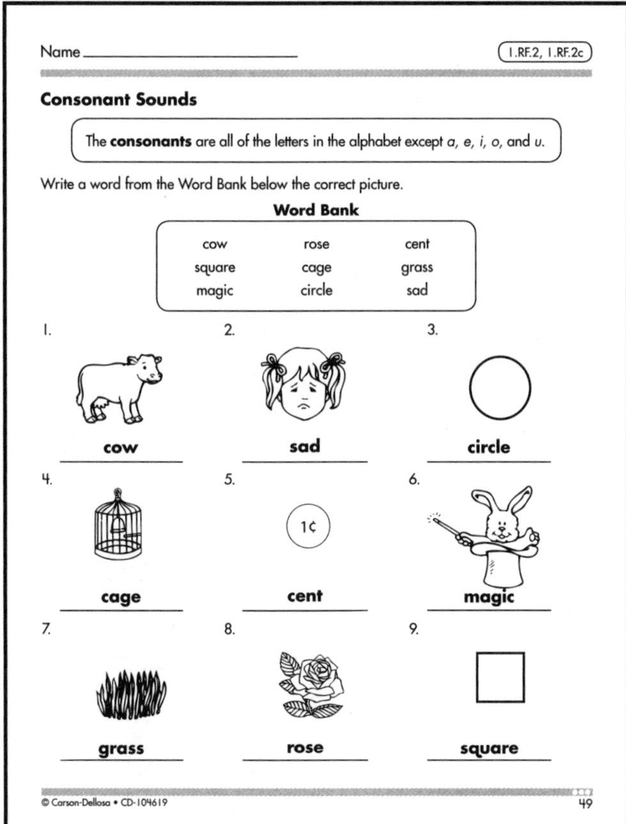

Name ______________ (1.RF.2, 1.RF.2c)

Consonant Sounds

The **consonants** are all of the letters in the alphabet except *a*, *e*, *i*, *o*, and *u*.

Write a word from the Word Bank below the correct picture.

Word Bank

cow	rose	cent
square	cage	grass
magic	circle	sad

1. cow
2. sad
3. circle
4. cage
5. cent
6. magic
7. grass
8. rose
9. square

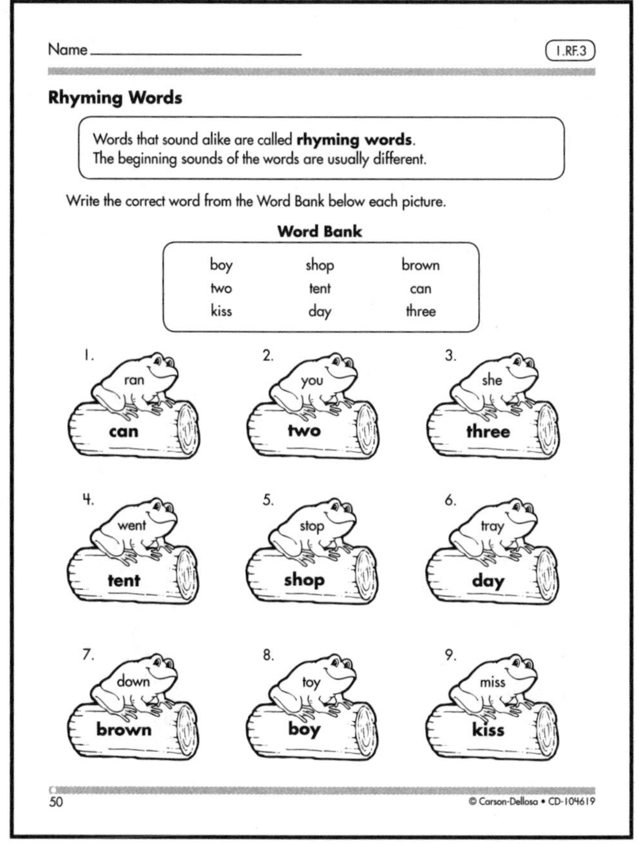

Name ______________ (1.RF.3)

Rhyming Words

Words that sound alike are called **rhyming words**.
The beginning sounds of the words are usually different.

Write the correct word from the Word Bank below each picture.

Word Bank

boy	shop	brown
two	tent	can
kiss	day	three

1. ran — can
2. you — two
3. she — three
4. went — tent
5. stop — shop
6. tray — day
7. down — brown
8. toy — boy
9. miss — kiss

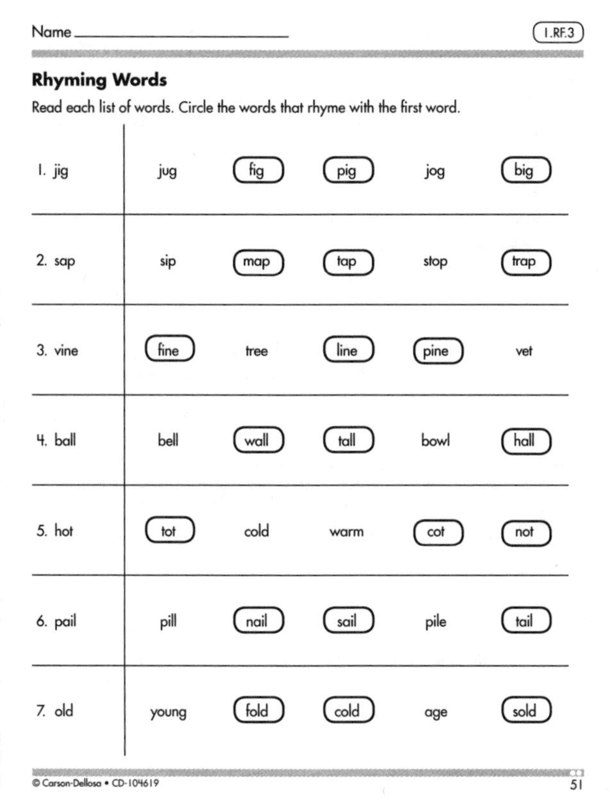

Name ______________ (1.RF.3)

Rhyming Words

Read each list of words. Circle the words that rhyme with the first word.

1. jig	jug	**fig**	**pig**	jog	**big**
2. sap	sip	**map**	**tap**	stop	**trap**
3. vine	**fine**	tree	**line**	**pine**	vet
4. ball	bell	**wall**	**tall**	bowl	**hall**
5. hot	**tot**	cold	warm	**cot**	**not**
6. pail	pill	**nail**	**sail**	pile	**tail**
7. old	young	**fold**	**cold**	age	**sold**

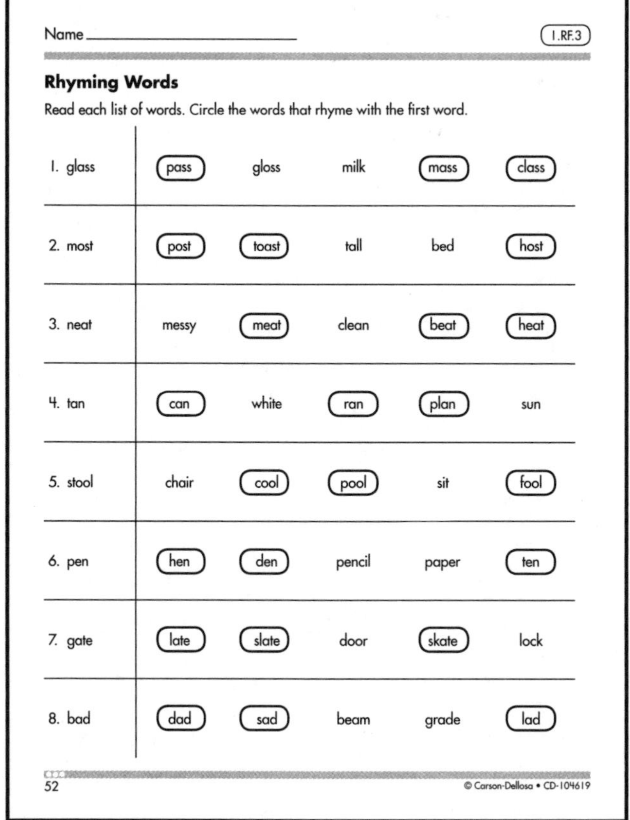

Name ______________ (1.RF.3)

Rhyming Words

Read each list of words. Circle the words that rhyme with the first word.

1. glass	**pass**	gloss	milk	**mass**	**class**
2. most	**post**	**toast**	tall	bed	**host**
3. neat	messy	**meat**	clean	**beat**	**heat**
4. tan	**can**	white	**ran**	**plan**	sun
5. stool	chair	**cool**	**pool**	sit	**fool**
6. pen	**hen**	**den**	pencil	paper	**ten**
7. gate	**late**	**slate**	door	**skate**	lock
8. bad	**dad**	**sad**	beam	grade	**lad**

Answer Key

Name ______________________ (1.RF.4, 1.RF.4a)

Accuracy and Fluency

Read the story.

Robin Hood

Robin Hood lived long ago in England. Robin Hood's king was named Richard. King Richard was away, so the sheriff was in charge. The sheriff was a terrible leader. He made the poor people even poorer. The rich people grew richer.

Robin Hood lived in the woods. He wanted to help the poor people. When the rich people drove through the woods, Robin Hood stole their money. He gave the money to the poor people.

Circle your answers.

1. Is Robin Hood alive today?
   yes **(no)**
2. Did Robin Hood like the man who was in charge?
   yes **(no)**
3. Who do you think might have been afraid of Robin Hood?
   poor people **(rich people)** thieves
4. Who do you think probably liked Robin Hood?
   (poor people) rich people thieves

Draw a line to help the rich man get through the woods without running into Robin Hood.

Name ______________________ (1.RF.4, 1.RF.4a)

Accuracy and Fluency

Read the story.

Chinese New Year

Chinese New Year is a happy holiday. It comes once a year. Chinese families around the world celebrate. The new year begins in January or February.

There is a colorful parade. The Chinese dragon dances in the parade. The dragon has a colorful head. One person carries the head. Many people carry the dragon's long, long tail. The dragon dances. It tries to catch money from the crowd.

Families get together on Chinese New Year. They set off fireworks. They eat lots of special foods. They eat dumplings. They eat cakes. Some people even eat jellyfish and giant meatballs. Most of all, the families just want to be together.

Circle fact or opinion.

1. Chinese New Year is a holiday. **(fact)** opinion
2. The parade is fun. fact **(opinion)**
3. The dragon dances in the parade. **(fact)** opinion
4. The food is wonderful. fact **(opinion)**
5. The dragon is the best part of the day. fact **(opinion)**

Name ______________________ (1.RF.4, 1.RF.4a)

Accuracy and Fluency

Read the story.

Ballet Class

Kira loves ballet class. She goes every Tuesday after school. Class lasts one hour. First, Kira and the other dancers stretch and warm up.

Next, the dancers must warm up their joints at the bar. They bend their legs and bodies. They put their feet in different positions. They hold onto the bar to balance. Kira is doing pliés (plee-ayz).

Then, Kira exercises without the bar. She dances in the room with her arms and legs. She is graceful and strong. Dance class is hard work. Her teacher walks around and helps the dancers. He shows Nathan how to hold his head straight. He shows Alice how to relax her shoulders. He teaches them all how to pull in their stomachs.

The next part of class is fun. Kira loves to jump and do pirouettes. They practice special steps and movements. They move with the music.

Kira wants to be a ballerina. She pays attention to her teacher. She knows that being a dancer is hard, but she loves it."

Circle your answers.

1. What does Kira love to do? paint pictures **(dance)** ride her bike
2. Which words describe Kira? fast runner **(hard worker)** colorful
3. What do you think Kira is like? **(good listener)** good writer good baby-sitter
4. What would Kira say about ballet class? too long **(really fun)** very noisy
5. What does Kira want to be when she grows up? a clown a dentist **(a ballerina)**

Name ______________________ (1.RF.4, 1.RF.4a, 1.RF.4b)

Accuracy and Fluency

Write your start time below. Read the story out loud. Then, write the time when you stop reading.

Start Time: __________

End Time: __________

How long did it take you to read the story? __________

Which words were difficult?

____

Read the story.

Skunk Perfume

Why do skunks smell so bad? Well, it's not actually the skunk that smells bad. It's the "perfume" the skunk sprays that smells. That cute little black-and-white animal does not have big teeth or claws to fight off its enemies. The only way to scare away its enemies is with a spray of skunk perfume.

When a big owl comes looking for a meal, the skunk stamps its feet. It puffs up its tail. This does not scare the owl. The skunk is just warning the enemy to stay away. If the warning does not work, the skunk turns around and sprays the owl. This stinky spray stings the owl's eyes. The owl smells this and flies away fast. Wasn't the skunk nice to give a warning first? Next time, the owl will watch out for that cute little black-and-white animal.

Reading times and words listed will vary.

Answer Key

Name ____________ (1.RF.4, 1.RF.4a, 1.RF.4b)

Accuracy and Fluency

Write your start time below. Read the story out loud. Then, write the time when you stop reading.

Start Time: ________

End Time: ________

How long did it take you to read the story? ________

Which words were difficult?

____

Read the story.

Charades

Have you ever played charades? Charades is a fun game to play with a large group of friends. All you need to play is a pencil and paper.

Split the group into two teams. Each team writes down book, movie, and song titles on little pieces of paper. The pieces of paper are then put into two bowls. One person takes a piece of paper from the other teams bowl. That person must act out the title. Her team has to guess what the title is.

First, the player shows the team whether it is a movie, song, or book. The player cannot talk or make sounds. Only hand and body motions are allowed. The player shows how many words are in the title. Then, the team watches the player act out the words. They guess and shout out their answers.

Everyone gets a turn. Both teams play. The winner is the team that guesses the most titles.

Reading times and words listed will vary.

Name ____________ (1.RF.4, 1.RF.4a, 1.RF.4b, 1.RI.10)

Accuracy and Fluency

Write your start time below. Read the story out loud. Then, write the time when you stop reading.

Start Time: ________

End Time: ________

How long did it take you to read the story? ________

Which words were difficult?

____

Read the story.

The Great Lakes

Stand on the sunny shore of Lake Michigan. Feel the sand between your toes. Hear the seagulls screaming. Look at the water. You can't see the other side of the lake! Is it an ocean? No, it is a Great Lake.

The five Great Lakes are not oceans. Their water is not salty. The Great Lakes are huge freshwater lakes.

Next to the lakes, there are sandy beaches, dunes, rocks, and cities. People play on the beaches, walk on the dunes, and go boating in the water. Many people use the water in their homes for drinking and washing. Others catch and eat the fish in the Great Lakes.

Since the Great Lakes are not salty, there are no sharks or whales. There are many different kinds of fish. There are also ducks, seagulls, and other birds. Seaweed grows in the water.

People must take care of the lakes. They are getting polluted. Trash is on the beaches. Oil is in the water. Chemicals and trash are in the water, too. This is bad for the many animals that live in the water. It is bad for the people that live around the water, too.

The Great Lakes are beautiful natural resources.

Reading times and words listed will vary.

Name ____________ (1.RL.10, 1.RF.4)

Accuracy and Fluency

Write your start time below. Read the story out loud. Then, write the time when you stop reading.

Start Time: ________

End Time: ________

How long did it take you to read the story? ________

Which words were difficult?

____

Read the story.

Magic Trick

"My name is Larry Houdini. Welcome to my magic show! Watch carefully as I make this coin disappear. I reach into my right pocket and take out a handful of coins. Now I take one quarter from the pile. I'll put the rest of the coins back in my pocket. Now I will tap my hand with a magic wand. Poof! The quarter is gone!"

Where did it go? Larry is a good magician. Larry can't really make coins disappear. He just makes you look somewhere else. You can do Larry's trick. The trick is that he never took the quarter! You try it. Make sure the back of your right hand faces the audience. Talk to the audience about what you are doing. Make your audience think you took a quarter from your right hand.

Reading times and words listed will vary.

Name ____________ (1.RF.4, 1.RF.4a, 1.RF.4b)

Accuracy and Fluency

Write your start time below. Read the story out loud. Then, write the time when you stop reading.

Start Time: ________

End Time: ________

How long did it take you to read the story? ________

Which words were difficult?

____

Read the story.

Making Bread

The two main ingredients in bread are flour and water. But, there are other important ingredients too. Yeast is very important. Without yeast, a loaf of bread would be flat. A little sugar or honey is needed to feed the yeast so that it will grow and make the bread fluffy. A little salt adds flavor to the bread. Butter or oil makes the bread tender and moist.

After the ingredients are mixed together, the bread dough is kneaded. To knead, you punch, push, fold, and pinch the dough. Kneading may take 15 minutes. The bread must rest in a warm place for an hour or two so that it can rise. Then, you can shape the bread into loaves. Before it bakes, the bread rises again until it is twice as big as when you started.

When bread is baking, the house smells wonderful. It is hard to wait until it is done!

Reading times and words listed will vary.

Answer Key

Name ______________________ (1.RI.10, 1.RF.4)

Accuracy and Fluency

Write your start time below. Read the story out loud. Then, write the time when you stop reading.

Start Time: ________

End Time: ________

How long did it take you to read the story? ________

Which words were difficult?

____

Read the story.

Yellowstone National Park

Yellowstone National Park bursts with sounds, sights, and smells. Yellowstone is the site of an old volcano. The bubbling hot water and shooting steam are heated from inside the earth. The first people who saw Yellowstone must have thought they were on the moon!

All is quiet. The air is still. Suddenly, water spurts out of the ground high into the air. Old Faithful is a famous geyser in Yellowstone Park. A geyser is a fountain of water that shoots from inside the earth. First, you hear hissing steam. Then, the sound is like forty showers. After several minutes, the fountain stops. All is quiet again.

The mud pots gurgle and glug. The gray mud bubbles in large, soupy ponds. The ponds smell like rotten eggs. You can feel the steamy heat around them.

Crystal clear pools are as hot as tea. The edge of the water is even with the ground. Sometimes, animals fall into the pools. They don't see them until they are too close. You can see bones in the bottom of some pools.

It is truly amazing to see the wonders of Yellowstone National Park.

Reading times and words listed will vary.

© Carson-Dellosa • CD-104619 61

Name ______________________ (1.W.1)

Writing an Opinion

Read the story.

Feeding the Dog

Luke has a pet dog named Kip. Luke feeds Kip every morning. He opens the back door and calls Kip. Kip runs to the door. Luke puts food in his bowl. Kip wags his tail and eats.

Answer the questions with complete sentences.

1. Is it hard to take care of a pet? **Answers will vary.**
2. Why do you think so?
3. Write another reason why it might be hard or easy to take care of a pet.
4. Who do you think enjoys taking care of pets?

62 © Carson-Dellosa • CD-104619

Name ______________________ (1.W.1)

Writing an Opinion

Read the story.

Cooking Soup

Clay is cooking soup. He puts a large pot on the stove. He opens a can of beans. Then, he opens a can of corn. He puts the food in the pot. Clay heats the soup. It will taste great!

Answer the questions with complete sentences.

1. Is it hard to make soup? **Answers will vary.**
2. Why do you think so?
3. Write another reason why it might be hard or easy to make soup.
4. Who do you think enjoys making soup?
5. What foods do you like to make?

© Carson-Dellosa • CD-104619 63

Name ______________________ (1.W.1)

Writing an Opinion

Read the story.

Washing Clothes

Ned needs to wash his dirty clothes. First, he sorts the colors. The white shirts go together. He puts the clothes in the washer. Then, he puts in the soap. When the clothes are clean, Ned puts them in the dryer.

Answer the questions with complete sentences.

Answers will vary.

1. Is it hard to wash clothes? ________
2. Why do you think so?
3. Write another reason why it might be hard or easy to wash clothes.
4. Who do you think enjoys washing clothes? ________
5. What other chores can a person do?
6. What chores do you like to do? ________
7. What chores do you dislike doing?

64 © Carson-Dellosa • CD-104619

Answer Key

Name ______________________ I.W.3

Writing about Yourself

Read the story.

Time for School

Cath is going to school for the first time. Mom tells her it is time to get up. Cath eats breakfast and brushes her teeth. She puts on a new dress. Mom helps her tie her shoes. She hands Cath a sack lunch. Then, she walks Cath to the bus stop.

Answer the questions with complete sentences.

1. Who helps you get ready for school in the morning? **Answers will vary.**
2. What do you do first when you get ready?
3. What do you do next?
4. What time do you get to school?

© Carson-Dellosa • CD-104619 65

Name ______________________ I.W.3

Writing about Yourself

Read the story.

Bedtime Story

Jon's father reads a story to him each night. Jon brushes his teeth. Then, he gets in bed, and his father sits in a chair. He reads a story and tells Jon good night. Jon dreams about the story.

Answer the questions with complete sentences.

1. Who reads you bedtime stories? **Answers will vary.**
2. What do you do before you start to read?
3. What do you do while you are reading together?
4. What do you do when you have finished reading?
5. What time do you fall asleep?

66 © Carson-Dellosa • CD-104619

Name ______________________ I.W.3

Writing about Yourself

Read the story.

Playing Tag

My friends and I played tag. We picked teams. Mimi was picked first. She is a good player. Rita ran fast in the game. It was hard to catch her. Then, Zeke hid behind a tree. We could not find him. We were tired at the end of the day. It was a fun day.

Answer the questions with complete sentences.

1. Who plays outdoor games with you? **Answers will vary.**
2. When do you play outdoors?
3. What game do you like to play together?
4. How do you play the game?
5. How does the game end?
6. What game do you want to play next?

© Carson-Dellosa • CD-104619 67

Name ______________________ I.W.3

Writing about Yourself

Read the story.

After School

Erin likes to go to Grandpa's after school. He picks her up at the school gate. They drive to his house. Erin hangs up her coat while Grandpa makes her a snack. She eats the food and then does her homework. Sometimes they watch TV!

Answer the questions with complete sentences.

1. Where do you go after school? **Answers will vary.**
2. What do you do first after school?
3. What do you do second after school?
4. When do you eat dinner?

68 © Carson-Dellosa • CD-104619

Answer Key

Name ______________________ (I.W.3)

Writing about Yourself

Read the story.

Zak's Sister

Zak has a baby sister. He helps take care of her on Saturdays. In the morning, he brushes her hair. In the afternoon, he makes funny faces so that she will laugh. In the evening, he feeds her. Then, he puts her to bed. Finally, Zak goes to bed. Zak's mom says Zak is a good big brother.

Answer the questions with complete sentences.

Answers will vary.

1. Do you take care of something or someone? ______________________
2. What do you take care of? ______________________
3. Why do you do first?
4. What do you do next?
5. What else do you take care of? ______________________
6. Why do you take care of this?

© Carson-Dellosa • CD-104619 69

Name ______________________ (I.W.3)

Writing about Yourself

Read the story.

Our Picnic

Our family went on a picnic in the park. My brother brought a friend. Dad cooked burgers on the grill. I made a salad. Mom served ice cream after we ate. After the ice cream, we played on the swings. Mom and Dad rested under the trees. Then, we went home.

Answer the questions with complete sentences.

1. What would you do to get ready to go on a picnic? **Answers will vary.**
2. What would you take to a picnic?
3. What would you do at the picnic?
4. Where would you play?
5. What game would you play first? ______________________
6. What game would you play next? ______________________
7. When would you go home?

70 © Carson-Dellosa • CD-104619

Name ______________________ (I.W.6, I.W.8)

Gathering Information

Read the story.

Picking a Puppy

Mom said I could get a pet. We went to the store. We looked at some puppies. A black one licked me. Then, a white one wagged her tail. It was hard to choose. We picked the little spotted puppy with the sad eyes. I will take good care of him.

Answer the questions with complete sentences.
Gather information from books and the computer.
Share your information with a friend.

Answers will vary.

1. Where do people get puppies?
2. Why do people want puppies?
3. What are two things a puppy needs?

© Carson-Dellosa • CD-104619 71

Name ______________________ (I.W.6, I.W.8)

Gathering Information

Read the story.

Emmy's Hamster

Emmy has a pet hamster. She takes good care of him. Every day she cleans his cage. Then, she feeds him grain and seeds. After that, she puts him on her lap and plays with him. She puts him back in his cage. He runs in a wheel. Emmy thinks hamsters are fun pets!

Answer the questions with complete sentences.
Gather information from books and the computer.
Share your information with a friend.

Answers will vary.

1. Where do people get hamsters?
2. Why do people want hamsters?
3. What do you need to take care of a hamster?
4. What are two things hamsters likes to do?

72 © Carson-Dellosa • CD-104619

Answer Key

Name ____________ (I.W.6, I.W.8)

Gathering Information

Read the story.

Lightning

The sky lights up with a flash. Crash! Thunder booms. Lightning is a very big electric spark. Thunder is the noise made by lightning.

Lightning happens during a storm. The dark clouds fill with a charge. The electricity in the clouds moves very fast to the ground. The path of the electricity is a bright streak of light. It is called lightning.

Lightning moves faster than its sound. When lightning is close, you hear the thunder at the same time. When lightning is far away, the thunder booms later. When you see lightning, count the seconds until the thunder. If you count five seconds, the lightning is one mile (1.6 km) away. If you count 10 seconds, the lightning is two miles (3.2 km) away.

Answer the questions with complete sentences. Gather information from books and the computer to help you. Share your information with a friend.

1. Why is lightning dangerous? **Answers will vary.**
2. What are two ways people can stay safe in an electrical storm?
3. Tell about a thunderstorm you have seen and heard.
4. In what season does lightning usually strike?

Name ____________ (I.L.1e)

Choosing Verbs

A **verb** is a word that shows action.
A verb can happen in the past, present, or future.

Read each sentence. Circle the correct verb to complete the sentence.

We **walked** to school. *(past)*
Maya **has** an art class. *(present)*
Jayson **will go** to his grandma's house. *(future)*

1. Ray ______ well. listen **(listens)**
2. She ______ to play tag. **(loves)** love
3. Sheri can ______ ten laps. swam **(swim)**
4. Jen ______ the circus show yesterday. will watch **(watched)**
5. He ______ the wet shirt and hung it up. **(dried)** will dry

Name ____________ (I.L.1e)

Choosing Verbs

A **verb** is a word that shows action.
A verb can happen in the past, present, or future.

Read each sentence. Circle the correct verb to complete the sentence.

1. My brother ______ in the park. **(played)** play
2. I ______ the last cookie. takes **(took)**
3. Phil ______ late. am **(was)**
4. Monkeys ______ me laugh. **(make)** makes
5. Trina ______ a blue ring. have **(has)**
6. Mom ______ her gold necklace yesterday. will wear **(wore)**
7. Pam ______ my best friend. are **(is)**

Name ____________ (I.L.1e)

Choosing Verbs

Read each sentence. Circle the correct verb to complete the sentence.

1. We ______ to draw. **(like)** likes
2. The dog ______ to her. run **(ran)**
3. Mr. Ang ______ a story after we ate. **(told)** will tell
4. I ______ Dad good-bye when he left. will hug **(hugged)**
5. That puppy ______ a lot. eat **(eats)**
6. The road ______ bumpy. **(was)** were
7. Her car ______ too slowly. **(goes)** go
8. Mark ______ his lunch. want **(wants)**
9. Lions can ______ really loudly. **(roar)** roared
10. We like to ______ in puddles. jumped **(jump)**

Answer Key

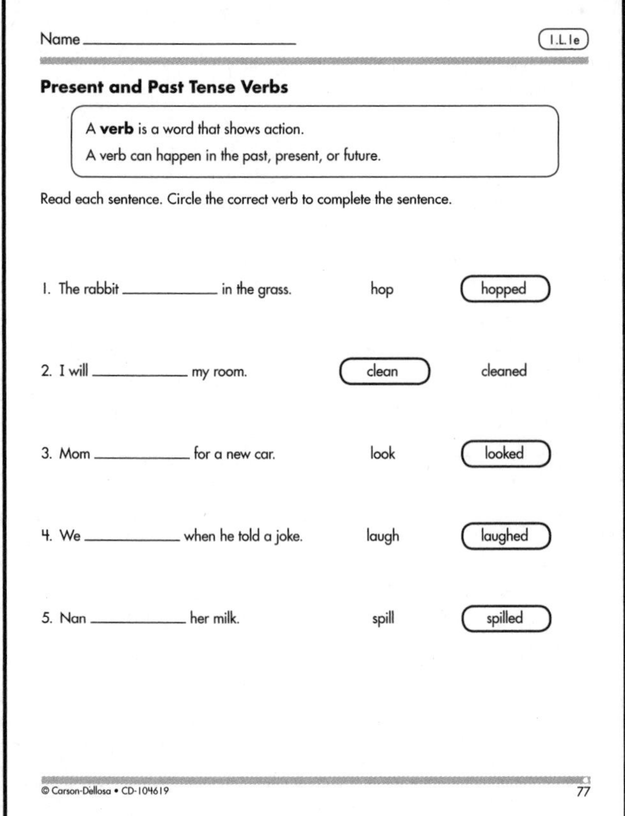

Name ________________ (1.L.1e)

Present and Past Tense Verbs

A **verb** is a word that shows action.
A verb can happen in the past, present, or future.

Read each sentence. Circle the correct verb to complete the sentence.

1. The rabbit ________ in the grass.	hop	(hopped)
2. I will ________ my room.	(clean)	cleaned
3. Mom ________ for a new car.	look	(looked)
4. We ________ when he told a joke.	laugh	(laughed)
5. Nan ________ her milk.	spill	(spilled)

© Carson-Dellosa • CD-104619 77

Name ________________ (1.L.1e)

Present and Past Tense Verbs

A **verb** is a word that shows action.
A verb can happen in the past, present, or future.

Read each sentence. Circle the correct verb to complete the sentence.

1. Please ________ the right answer.	(circle)	circled
2. Dad ________ at the lake.	fish	(fished)
3. Mike ________ to school this morning.	walk	(walked)
4. I ________ the ball to her a minute ago.	roll	(rolled)
5. Kate ________ her car last week.	fix	(fixed)
6. Grandma ________ carefully onto the ladder.	step	(stepped)
7. She ________ the dog on the head.	pat	(patted)

78 © Carson-Dellosa • CD-104619

Name ________________ (1.L.1e)

Present and Past Tense Verbs

A **verb** is a word that shows action.
A verb can happen in the past, present, or future.

Read each sentence. Circle the correct verb to complete the sentence.

1. I like to ________ to the store.	(walk)	walked
2. Matt ________ off the high board.	jump	(jumped)
3. We want to ________ down the river.	(row)	rowed
4. Please ________ your work.	(finish)	finished
5. Pete ________ breakfast yesterday.	cook	(cooked)
6. We will ________ to play soccer.	(learn)	learned
7. Mary ________ down the sidewalk.	skip	(skipped)
8. Please ________ to the next chair.	(move)	moved
9. My sister ________ to me when I walked by.	wave	(waved)
10. We ________ baseball last Saturday.	(played)	play

© Carson-Dellosa • CD-104619 79

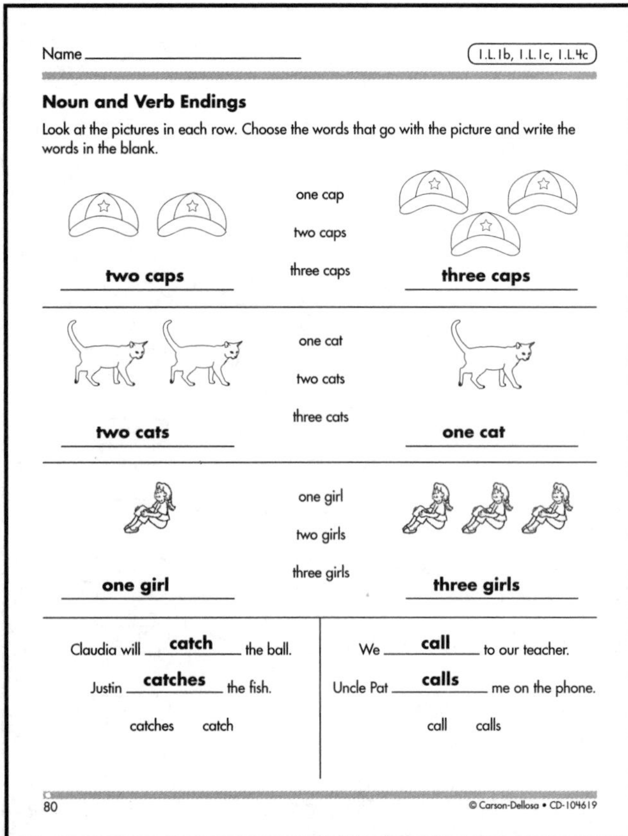

Name ________________ (1.L.1b, 1.L.1c, 1.L.4c)

Noun and Verb Endings

Look at the pictures in each row. Choose the words that go with the picture and write the words in the blank.

two caps	one cap / two caps / three caps	**three caps**
two cats	one cat / two cats / three cats	**one cat**
one girl	one girl / two girls / three girls	**three girls**

Claudia will **catch** the ball.
Justin **catches** the fish.
catches catch

We **call** to our teacher.
Uncle Pat **calls** me on the phone.
call calls

80 © Carson-Dellosa • CD-104619

Answer Key

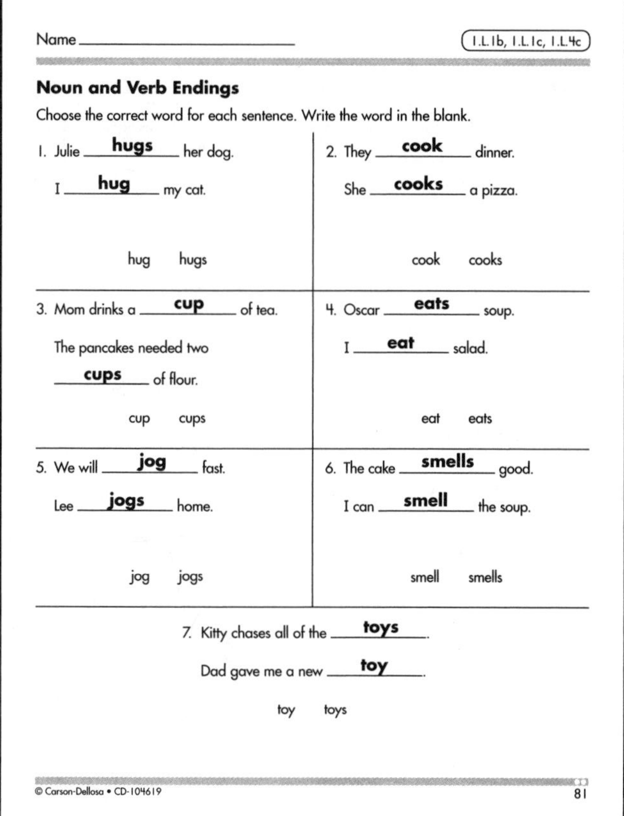

Name ____________ (1.L.1b, 1.L.1c, 1.L.4c)

Noun and Verb Endings

Choose the correct word for each sentence. Write the word in the blank.

1. Julie **hugs** her dog.
   I **hug** my cat.
   hug hugs

2. They **cook** dinner.
   She **cooks** a pizza.
   cook cooks

3. Mom drinks a **cup** of tea.
   The pancakes needed two **cups** of flour.
   cup cups

4. Oscar **eats** soup.
   I **eat** salad.
   eat eats

5. We will **jog** fast.
   Lee **jogs** home.
   jog jogs

6. The cake **smells** good.
   I can **smell** the soup.
   smell smells

7. Kitty chases all of the **toys**.
   Dad gave me a new **toy**.
   toy toys

Name ____________ (1.L.1b, 1.L.1c, 1.L.4c)

Noun and Verb Endings

Choose the correct word for each sentence. Write the word in the blank.

1. My **fish** is in a bowl.
   Dad **fishes** in the pond.
   fish fishes

2. She **goes** to school.
   They **go** to work.
   go goes

3. Please get my **watch**.
   Mom bought two new **watches**.
   watch watches

4. Mom **coaches** our team.
   I **coach** my little sister.
   coach coaches

5. I will **fix** the problem.
   Jean **fixes** her bike.
   fix fixes

6. Tia rides her **bike** to school.
   I have three **bikes** in the garage.
   bike bikes

7. I will **brush** my hair.
   Peg **brushes** her hair often.
   brush brushes

8. Sandy visited many **beaches**.
   I will go to the **beach** tomorrow.
   beach beaches

Name ____________ (1.L.1b)

Introduction to Nouns

Nouns are words that name people, places, or things.

Which nouns could you find in your desk at school? Draw a line from these nouns to the desk.

ruler, birds, chalk, paper, stinky, tiger, skipping, path, green, hard, crayon, lion, cage, soft, pencil, cold, book, lizard, scissors, elephant

Name ____________ (1.L.1b)

Introduction to Nouns

Nouns are words that name people, places, or things.

Underline the nouns.

1. Kira has a yellow sun on her shirt.
2. Chase went to the store to buy apples.
3. Her brother watered the plants on the deck.
4. Sabena placed the cupcakes on the counter.
5. The bike on the sidewalk belongs to my friend.

Choose two nouns from the sentences that name things. Draw a picture of each one. Write their names.

6. ____________ 7. ____________

Answers will vary.

Answer Key

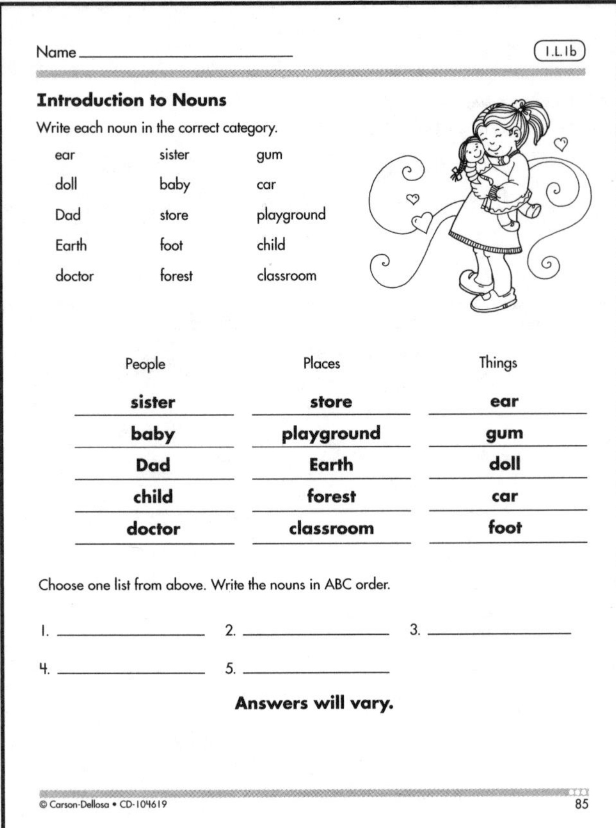

Name ____________________ I.L.1b

Introduction to Nouns

Write each noun in the correct category.

ear	sister	gum
doll	baby	car
Dad	store	playground
Earth	foot	child
doctor	forest	classroom

People	Places	Things
sister	**store**	**ear**
baby	**playground**	**gum**
Dad	**Earth**	**doll**
child	**forest**	**car**
doctor	**classroom**	**foot**

Choose one list from above. Write the nouns in ABC order.

1. ________ 2. ________ 3. ________

4. ________ 5. ________

Answers will vary.

© Carson-Dellosa • CD-104619 85

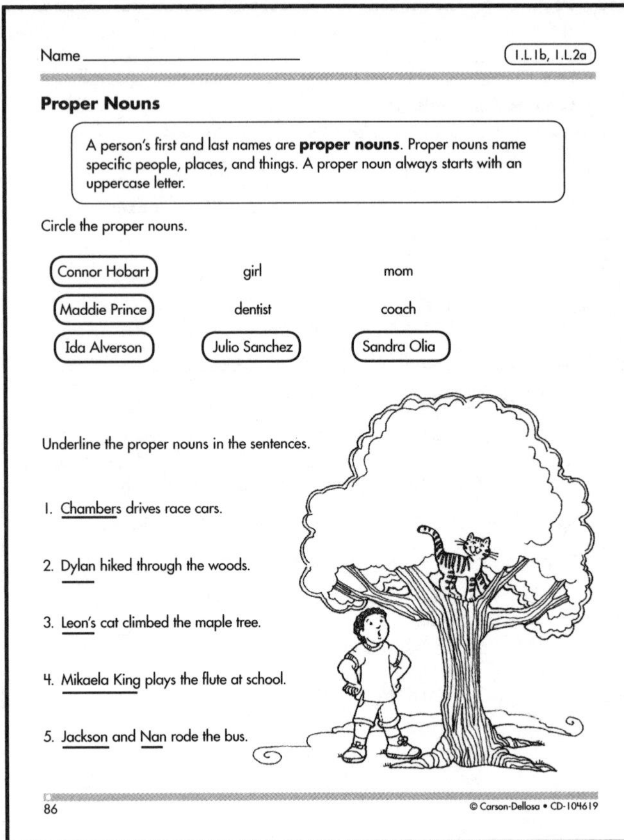

Name ____________________ I.L.1b, I.L.2a

Proper Nouns

A person's first and last names are **proper nouns**. Proper nouns name specific people, places, and things. A proper noun always starts with an uppercase letter.

Circle the proper nouns.

Connor Hobart	girl	mom
Maddie Prince	dentist	coach
Ida Alverson	Julio Sanchez	Sandra Olia

Underline the proper nouns in the sentences.

1. Chambers drives race cars.
2. Dylan hiked through the woods.
3. Leon's cat climbed the maple tree.
4. Mikaela King plays the flute at school.
5. Jackson and Nan rode the bus.

86 © Carson-Dellosa • CD-104619

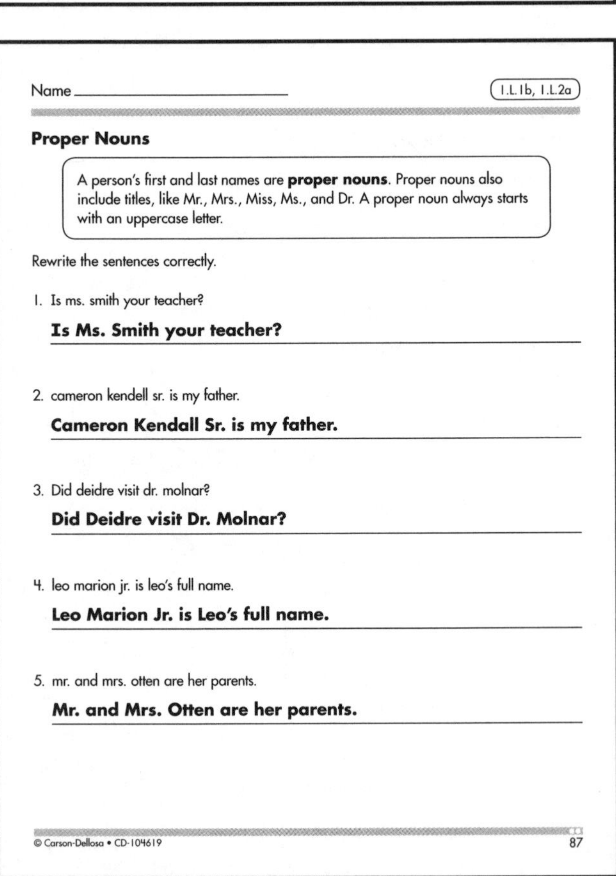

Name ____________________ I.L.1b, I.L.2a

Proper Nouns

A person's first and last names are **proper nouns**. Proper nouns also include titles, like Mr., Mrs., Miss, Ms., and Dr. A proper noun always starts with an uppercase letter.

Rewrite the sentences correctly.

1. Is ms. smith your teacher?
   Is Ms. Smith your teacher?
2. cameron kendell sr. is my father.
   Cameron Kendall Sr. is my father.
3. Did deidre visit dr. molnar?
   Did Deidre visit Dr. Molnar?
4. leo marion jr. is leo's full name.
   Leo Marion Jr. is Leo's full name.
5. mr. and mrs. otten are her parents.
   Mr. and Mrs. Otten are her parents.

© Carson-Dellosa • CD-104619 87

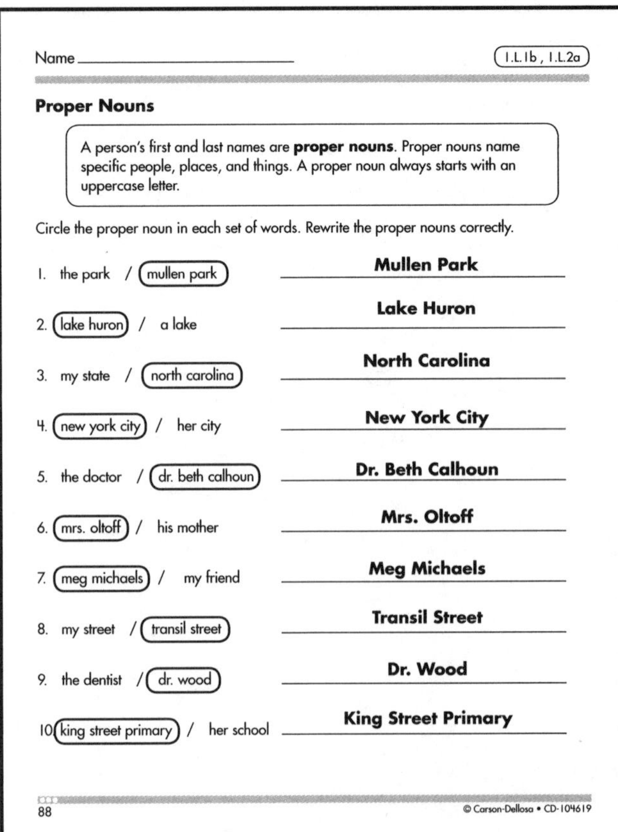

Name ____________________ I.L.1b, I.L.2a

Proper Nouns

A person's first and last names are **proper nouns**. Proper nouns name specific people, places, and things. A proper noun always starts with an uppercase letter.

Circle the proper noun in each set of words. Rewrite the proper nouns correctly.

1. the park / mullen park — **Mullen Park**
2. lake huron / a lake — **Lake Huron**
3. my state / north carolina — **North Carolina**
4. new york city / her city — **New York City**
5. the doctor / dr. beth calhoun — **Dr. Beth Calhoun**
6. mrs. oltoff / his mother — **Mrs. Oltoff**
7. meg michaels / my friend — **Meg Michaels**
8. my street / transil street — **Transil Street**
9. the dentist / dr. wood — **Dr. Wood**
10. king street primary / her school — **King Street Primary**

88 © Carson-Dellosa • CD-104619

Answer Key

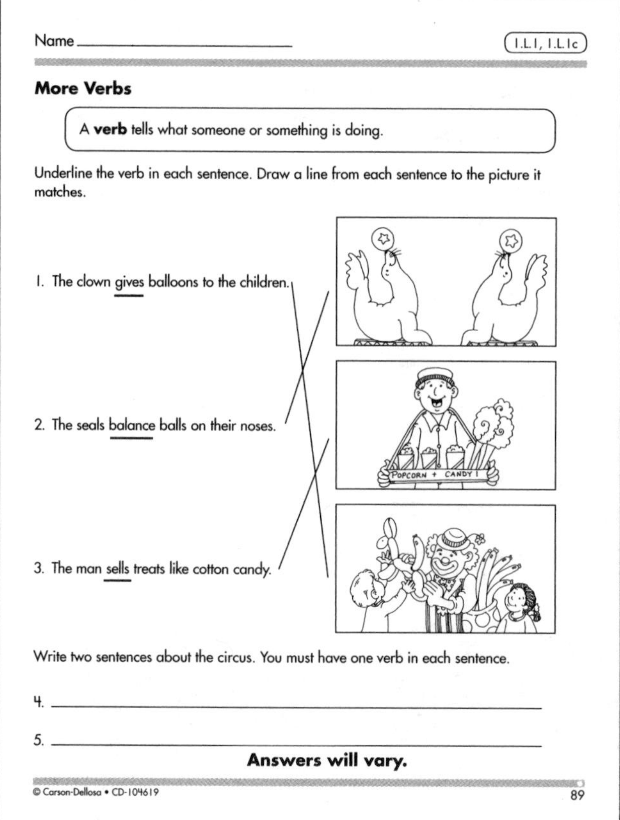

Name ____________________ I.L.1, I.L.1c

More Verbs

A **verb** tells what someone or something is doing.

Underline the verb in each sentence. Draw a line from each sentence to the picture it matches.

1. The clown gives balloons to the children.
2. The seals balance balls on their noses.
3. The man sells treats like cotton candy.

Write two sentences about the circus. You must have one verb in each sentence.

4. ____________________
5. ____________________

Answers will vary.

© Carson-Dellosa • CD-104619 89

Name ____________________ I.L.1, I.L.1c

More Verbs

A **verb** tells what someone or something is doing.
Example: *The boy **swings** the golf club.*

Underline the verb in each sentence.

1. My sister Emily slides down the slide.
2. My dad pushes Paige on the merry-go-round.
3. My brother Hal climbs the big tree.
4. My grandmother sits on the bench.
5. My grandfather hits the ball with a racket.
6. My mom catches Emily at the bottom.
7. I swing across the monkey bars.

90 © Carson-Dellosa • CD-104619

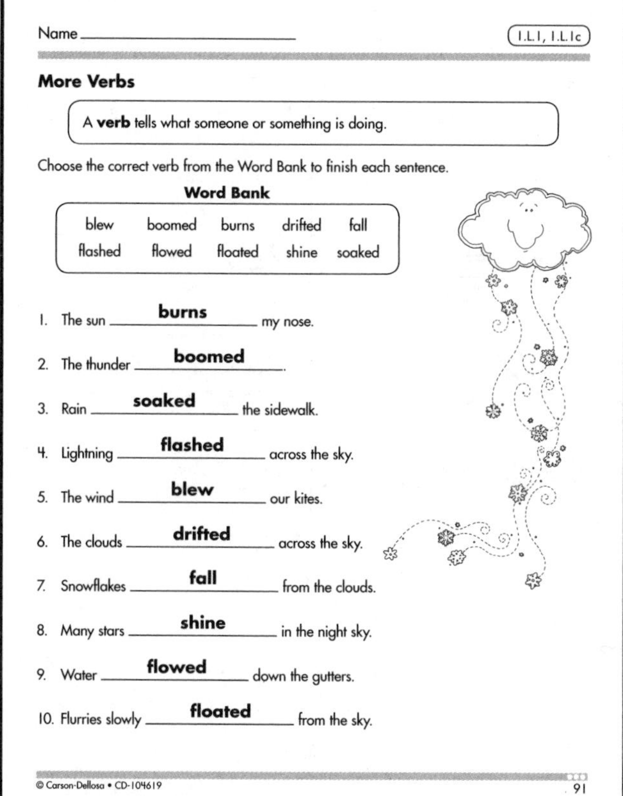

Name ____________________ I.L.1, I.L.1c

More Verbs

A **verb** tells what someone or something is doing.

Choose the correct verb from the Word Bank to finish each sentence.

Word Bank

blew	boomed	burns	drifted	fall
flashed	flowed	floated	shine	soaked

1. The sun **burns** my nose.
2. The thunder **boomed**.
3. Rain **soaked** the sidewalk.
4. Lightning **flashed** across the sky.
5. The wind **blew** our kites.
6. The clouds **drifted** across the sky.
7. Snowflakes **fall** from the clouds.
8. Many stars **shine** in the night sky.
9. Water **flowed** down the gutters.
10. Flurries slowly **floated** from the sky.

© Carson-Dellosa • CD-104619 91

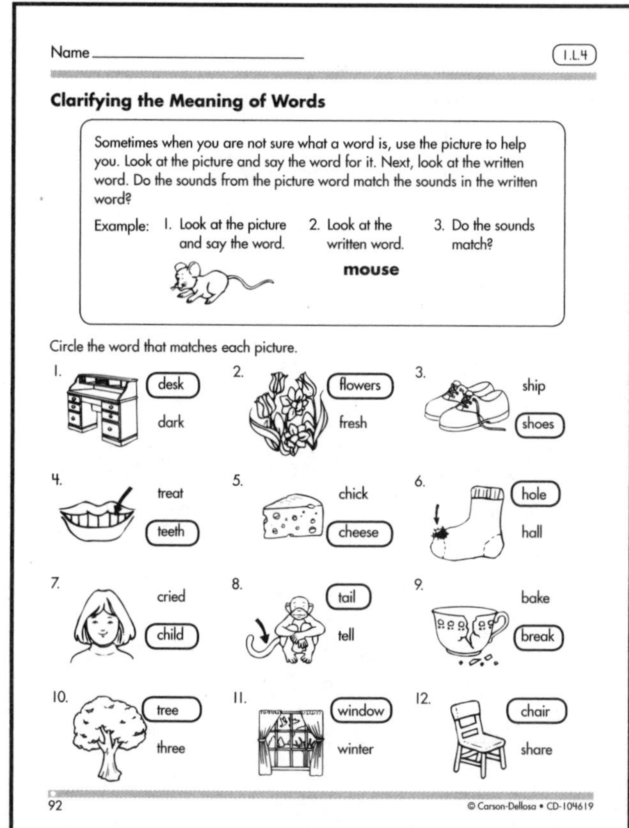

Name ____________________ I.L.4

Clarifying the Meaning of Words

Sometimes when you are not sure what a word is, use the picture to help you. Look at the picture and say the word for it. Next, look at the written word. Do the sounds from the picture word match the sounds in the written word?

Example: 1. Look at the picture and say the word. 2. Look at the written word. 3. Do the sounds match?

mouse

Circle the word that matches each picture.

1. desk / dark — (desk)
2. flowers / fresh — (flowers)
3. ship / shoes — (shoes)
4. treat / teeth — (teeth)
5. chick / cheese — (cheese)
6. hole / hall — (hole)
7. cried / child — (child)
8. tail / tell — (tail)
9. bake / break — (break)
10. tree / three — (tree)
11. window / winter — (window)
12. chair / share — (chair)

92 © Carson-Dellosa • CD-104619

Answer Key

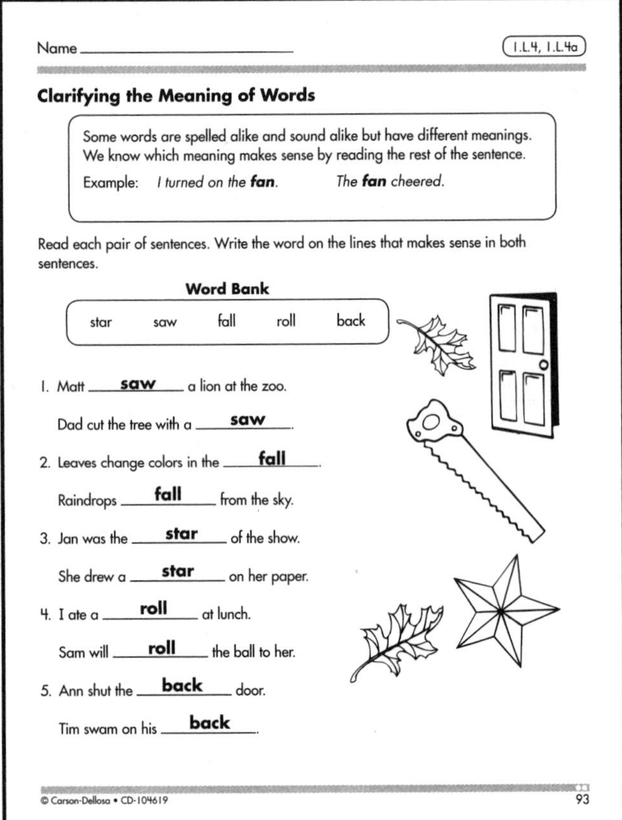

Name ____________ (1.L.4, 1.L.4a)

Clarifying the Meaning of Words

Some words are spelled alike and sound alike but have different meanings. We know which meaning makes sense by reading the rest of the sentence.

Example: *I turned on the **fan**.* *The **fan** cheered.*

Read each pair of sentences. Write the word on the lines that makes sense in both sentences.

Word Bank

star saw fall roll back

1. Matt **saw** a lion at the zoo.
   Dad cut the tree with a **saw**.
2. Leaves change colors in the **fall**.
   Raindrops **fall** from the sky.
3. Jan was the **star** of the show.
   She drew a **star** on her paper.
4. I ate a **roll** at lunch.
   Sam will **roll** the ball to her.
5. Ann shut the **back** door.
   Tim swam on his **back**.

© Carson-Dellosa • CD-104619 93

Name ____________ (1.L.4, 1.L.4a)

Clarifying the Meaning of Words

Use clues in each sentence to figure out the meaning of the underlined nonsense word. Circle the meaning of the word.

1. I use xapt to clean.
   fast (soap) time
2. The zoto hopped in the grass.
   (rabbit) doll car
3. We planted kibd in the garden.
   ducks boys (seeds)
4. There is a cefl in the sky.
   door (cloud) tree
5. We rode our huvot to the park.
   (bikes) house ball
6. You must japc your room.
   jump sleep (clean)
7. She went to a birthday leehm.
   (party) bath plant
8. The cat is niacp the basket.
   sing blow (under)

94 © Carson-Dellosa • CD-104619

Name ____________ (1.L.5b)

Categorizing Words

Things can be grouped together because they are alike in some way.

Example: These could be classified as a group of bugs.

Choose a group name from the Word Bank for each picture. Write it on the line.

Word Bank

pets shapes things that go
things to eat farm animals tools

1. **farm animals**
2. **things that go**
3. **things to eat**
4. **shapes**
5. **pets**
6. **tools**

© Carson-Dellosa • CD-104619 95

Name ____________ (1.L.5b)

Categorizing Words

Read the clues for each riddle. Think about the attributes. Circle the best answer.

1. I am long.
   I have a point.
   I help you write.
   What am I?
   arrow straw
   stick (pencil)
2. I can fly.
   I have pretty wings.
   I sip from flowers.
   What am I?
   (butterfly) airplane
   crow bee
3. I am orange.
   I am round.
   I have a green stem.
   What am I?
   (pumpkin) basketball
   dish sign
4. I climb trees.
   I make funny faces.
   I hang by my tail.
   What am I?
   raccoon bat
   (monkey) squirrel
5. I have two wheels.
   I can go fast.
   Children can ride me.
   What am I?
   car truck
   (bike) motorcycle

96 © Carson-Dellosa • CD-104619

Answer Key

Name ____________________ I.L.5b

Categorizing Words

Read the clues for each riddle. Think about the attributes. Circle the best answer.

1. I am brown or gray.
I have a big tail.
I eat acorns.
What am I?

kangaroo mouse
bear **squirrel**

2. I am round.
I can be many colors.
I help you see.
What am I?

eyes wheels
earrings circles

3. I have four legs.
I am made of wood or metal.
I belong at a table.
What am I?

chair animal
stool couch

4. I am very large.
I can swim.
I live in the sea.
What am I?

ship crab
whale fish

5. I am soft.
I have sheets.
I help you rest.
What am I?

sofa pillow
bed blanket

6. I am fluffy.
I am found in the sky.
I can be white, gray, or black.
What am I?

cloud bird
moon balloon

© Carson-Dellosa • CD-104619 97

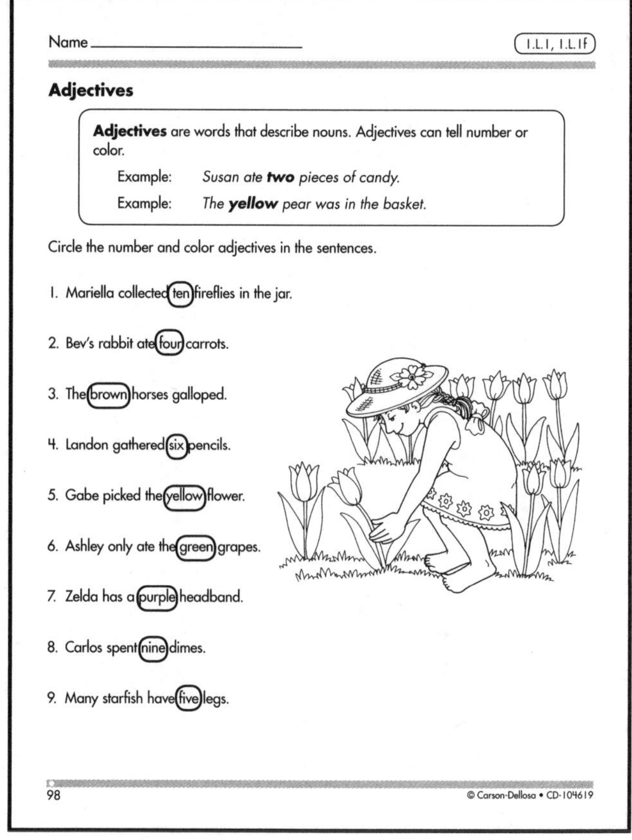
Name ____________________ I.L.1, I.L.1f

Adjectives

Adjectives are words that describe nouns. Adjectives can tell number or color.

Example: *Susan ate **two** pieces of candy.*
Example: *The **yellow** pear was in the basket.*

Circle the number and color adjectives in the sentences.

1. Mariella collected **ten** fireflies in the jar.
2. Bev's rabbit ate **four** carrots.
3. The **brown** horses galloped.
4. Landon gathered **six** pencils.
5. Gabe picked the **yellow** flower.
6. Ashley only ate the **green** grapes.
7. Zelda has a **purple** headband.
8. Carlos spent **nine** dimes.
9. Many starfish have **five** legs.

98 © Carson-Dellosa • CD-104619

Name ____________________ I.L.1, I.L.1f

Adjectives

Adjectives are words that describe nouns. Adjectives can tell size or shape.

Example: *Jillian bought the **square** picture frame.*
Example: *The **little** boy climbed the rope.*

Circle the size and shape adjectives in the sentences.

1. The **circular** clock is in the hallway.
2. Vinny washed the **square** window.
3. Carrie bought the **thin** ribbon.
4. Look at that **small** sand castle.
5. Yuri has an **oval** skateboard.
6. Get the dog's **long** leash.
7. Terrell caught a **tiny** fish!
8. Hannah found her **round** glasses.
9. Mae's **big** bucket is full of sand.
10. That **large** spider escaped from its cage!

© Carson-Dellosa • CD-104619 99

Name ____________________ I.L.1, I.L.1f

Adjectives

Adjectives are words that describe nouns. Adjectives can tell number, color, size, shape, or anything that adds detail.

Circle the adjectives.

1. **heavy** walked **old** house **loose** book shoe
2. **nine** sneezed **dry** star **broken** sing whale
3. **silly** **hairy** **blue** school **strong** tasty **wrinkled**
4. **gold** wiggle **new** **awful** friend **tired** blink

Use the adjectives to finish the sentences.
Or, write your own adjectives on the lines.

5. Whitney held the ____________________ snake.
6. Jo broke that ____________________ lamp.
7. Charlie tried to lift the ____________________ lamb.
8. Bailey rode his ____________________ scooter.
9. Layla wanted the ____________________ food on the menu.

Answers will vary.

100 © Carson-Dellosa • CD-104619

Answer Key

Name ____________________ (1.L.2, 1.L.2c)

Commas

> A **comma** is a type of punctuation mark used to separate a group of three or more words in a list or series.
>
> Example: *Sal ate and **soup** for lunch.*

Put commas between the words in each series.

1. Tim went fishing on Wednesday, Friday, Saturday, and Monday.
2. Ahmad, Spencer, Reese, and Jeremy played soccer.
3. Garrett, Faith, Justin, and I drove to the festival.
4. The fair had rides, food, animals, and games.
5. George likes to play with Zack, Tommy, Cole, and me.
6. Antoine's favorite subjects are math, reading, and science.
7. Perry has relatives in Florida, Indiana, and Tennessee.

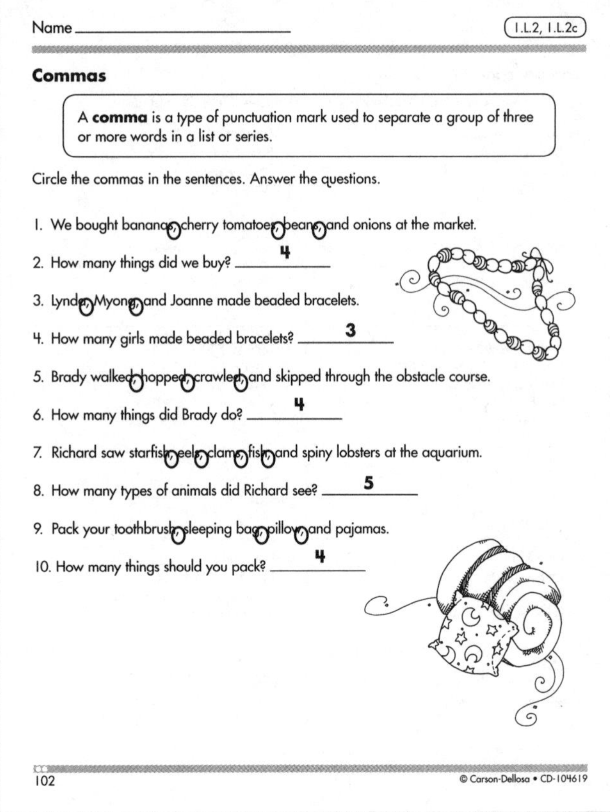

Name ____________________ (1.L.2, 1.L.2c)

Commas

> A **comma** is a type of punctuation mark used to separate a group of three or more words in a list or series.

Circle the commas in the sentences. Answer the questions.

1. We bought bananas, cherry tomatoes, beans, and onions at the market.
2. How many things did we buy? **4**
3. Lynda, Myong, and Joanne made beaded bracelets.
4. How many girls made beaded bracelets? **3**
5. Brady walked, hopped, crawled, and skipped through the obstacle course.
6. How many things did Brady do? **4**
7. Richard saw starfish, eels, clams, fish, and spiny lobsters at the aquarium.
8. How many types of animals did Richard see? **5**
9. Pack your toothbrush, sleeping bag, pillow, and pajamas.
10. How many things should you pack? **4**

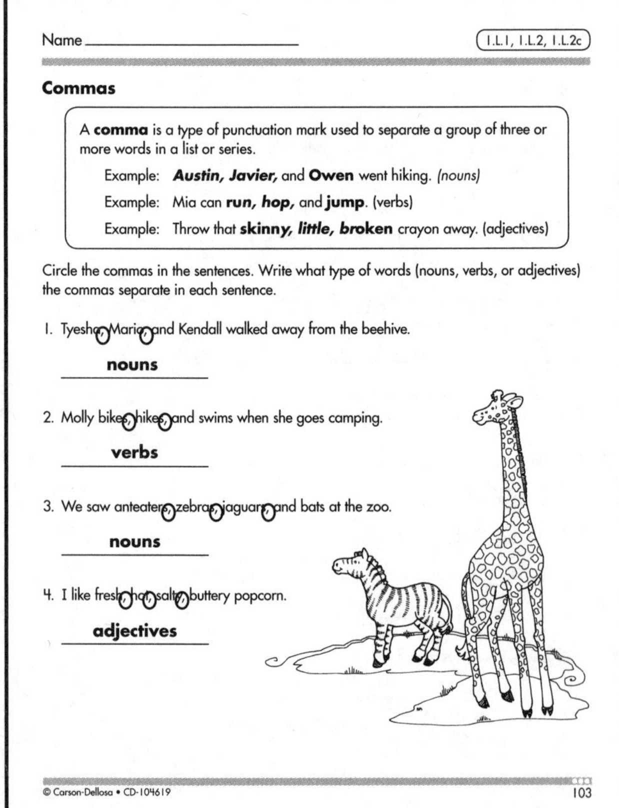

Name ____________________ (1.L.1, 1.L.2, 1.L.2c)

Commas

> A **comma** is a type of punctuation mark used to separate a group of three or more words in a list or series.
>
> Example: ***Austin, Javier,*** and **Owen** went hiking. *(nouns)*
>
> Example: Mia can ***run, hop,*** and **jump**. (verbs)
>
> Example: Throw that ***skinny, little, broken*** crayon away. (adjectives)

Circle the commas in the sentences. Write what type of words (nouns, verbs, or adjectives) the commas separate in each sentence.

1. Tyesha, Maria, and Kendall walked away from the beehive.

   nouns
2. Molly bikes, hikes, and swims when she goes camping.

   verbs
3. We saw anteaters, zebras, jaguars, and bats at the zoo.

   nouns
4. I like fresh, hot, salty, buttery popcorn.

   adjectives

Congratulations!

____

receives this award for

____

Signed ____________________ **Date** __________

afraid	always	angry	aunt
balloon	basketball	beautiful	box
breakfast	bright	butterfly	cage
careful	catch	climb	clock

clown © CD	coat © CD	crown © CD	different © CD
dolphin © CD	earth © CD	elephant © CD	fence © CD
finger © CD	flower © CD	fly © CD	fold © CD
forest © CD	fork © CD	funny © CD	glue © CD

great © CD	guard © CD	hamster © CD	honk © CD
huge © CD	jeans © CD	joke © CD	king © CD
kitten © CD	knife © CD	lion © CD	leaf © CD
mail © CD	milk © CD	morning © CD	neat © CD

necklace	night	ocean	open
pair	parrot	pencil	piece
plant	point	pretty	quick
return	ring	round	roll

scare	scream	shark	shell
shovel	shut	snake	special
squirrel	stove	study	swing
taste	teacher	thank	thick

thin 	thought 	throw 	together
truck 	uncle 	vine 	visit
wag 	warm 	watch 	wave
whisper 	wide 	wood 	young